DANTE'S DANCE:
ALL FOR AN AMEN

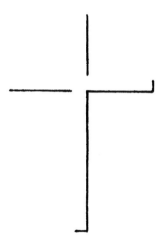

By Chris Meehan
and Jackie Venegas

Chapbook Press

Chapbook Press
Schuler Books
2660 28th Street SE
Grand Rapids, MI 49512
(616) 942-7330
www.schulerbooks.com

Printed at Schuler Books in Grand Rapids, MI on the Espresso Book Machine®

Copyright © 2011 by Jackie Venegas.

ISBN 13: 978-1-936243-29-7
ISBN 10: 01-936243-29-6

Scripture quotations labeled KJV are from the King James Version of the Bible.

Scripture quotations labeled NIV are from the Holy Bible, New International Version®. NIV®. Copyright © 1973, 1978, 1984, 2011 by Biblica, Inc.™ Used by permission of Zondervan. All rights reserved worldwide. www.zondervan.com.

Scripture quotations labeled NLT are from the Holy Bible, New Living Translation, copyright © 1996, 2004, 2007 by Tyndale House Foundation. Used by permission of Tyndale House Publishers, Inc., Carol Stream, Illinois 60188. All rights reserved.

The Silent Sound of Needles by Michael Zwerin. Prentice Hall 1969.

Brave New World by Aldous Huxley. Bantam Books, Inc. 1932, 1946.

Cover photo copyright by Steve Wolf.

DEDICATION

In loving memory of Reverend Dante Alighieri Venegas who chose this verse as an introduction to his biography.

> "Then the man in linen clothing, who carried the writer's case, reported back and said: 'I have finished the work you gave me to do.'" *Ezekiel 9:11 (NLT)*

Rev. Dante A. Venegas

DANTE'S DANCE:
ALL FOR AN AMEN

"I can dance on many sets."

D. A. V.

"Let all God's people say Amen."

D. A. V.

CONTENTS

The Story

	Introduction by Chris Meehan	7
1	Family History	11
2	Early Years	16
3	School Days	20
4	Home	24
5	"Pop"	28
6	Friends	33
7	God Was Watching	36
8	Behind Bars	39
9	Doing Time	41
10	"Am I Worth Something?"	44
11	Spiritual Reality	46
12	Not Ready Yet	49
13	"I'm Not Guilty!"	55
14	"To Whom It May Concern"	59
15	Change	65
16	"Buy a Ticket"	68
17	"Go Home"	70
18	Church	72
19	Small Beginnings	74
20	Pastrami	76
21	Jackie	78
22	Linked by God	80
23	Dante's Example	83
24	Strong Messages	86

25 Answered Prayers	89
26 Madison Square CRC	91
27 Challenges	94
28 Outreach	96
29 Lessons	98
30 Changed Lives	101
31 Ordination	104
32 "We've Come This Far by Faith"	108
33 Pastor Dante and Pastor Dave	112
34 From the Pulpit	115
35 Memories	118
36 Mentoring	122
37 Sabbatical	126
38 Stepping Down	130
39 Following His Heart	134
40 City Hope	136
41 Threatening Calls	139
42 Resilience	141
43 The Diagnosis	143
44 The Past Intrudes	145
45 "I Know the Lord Is Healing Me"	149
46 Time to Leave	153
47 "I Will Trust in the Lord until I Die"	156
48 All for an Amen	158
49 A Wife's Reflections: Wings and Roots	163

More Dante

Timeline	174
Writings	176
Poetry	185
Danteisms	192
Acknowledgments	200

INTRODUCTION

Held in a large undenominational church in Grand Rapids, Michigan on April 20, 2007, the Memorial Service for Rev. Dante Alighieri Venegas, better known as Pastor Dante, was by many accounts an "awe-inspiring event." Since I was there, I can attest to it.

Grace and holiness and a wonderful sense of serendipity filled the sanctuary, as did the voices of so many people who knew and loved this man, named after the famous 13th Century poet. Although there were many tears as his family and friends wheeled the 73-year-old pastor's coffin up to the front of the sanctuary, it was mostly a time of celebration. Hundreds of people—from different churches, denominations, ethnic groups, races, and social classes—filled the pews for the early evening service.

Many called themselves the sons and daughters of Dante, reflecting his spiritual influence on their lives and the inspiration he had provided them. They sat and listened as fellow pastors, friends and his daughters celebrated the life of this Christian Reformed Church minister who grew up as a heroin addict on the streets of New York City. It was an occasion recounting a truly amazing life that was turned around during a dramatic conversion experience in Bronx County Jail, which today is the site, oddly enough, of the new Yankee Stadium. There was even an audio clip of Dante preaching in his unmistakable voice—a sonorous voice that seemed to mix his spirited personality with a hint of humor as well as the deep baritones of the complex life he had led.

I didn't really know Dante when I was religion editor of the *Grand Rapids Press* in the 1980s. We met once, briefly. But I had heard of him, and that as a pastor of Madison Square Christian Reformed Church he was breaking ground in the CRC, which has its U.S. office in Grand Rapids and is an important denomination in West Michigan. Then, providentially, I got an email from

James Haveman, former director of the Michigan Department of Community Health. It was the same day in March of 2007 that I was leaving the newspaper business after nearly 30 years as a reporter, many of them spent covering religion. Haveman's email was as simple as it was surprising. Jim, whom I knew from my newspaper work, wanted me to talk to Dante, who was in a local Hospice, to see if maybe I could write something about the minister and what he meant to the denomination. Dante, Jim said, had an important story to tell—a story with many themes, beginning in New York City and ending in Grand Rapids.

Still, I wondered: Would this be a story that resonated beyond the people who knew Dante? I wasn't sure. I would later learn that it does have a wider reach, especially in the areas of race relations, multicultural ministry and ultimately the hope we find in Jesus Christ. The early part of Dante's story is rugged, grizzly, and tells a tale of being in six jails and prisons as part of his mighty struggle with drug addiction. But Dante's life can be a lesson in overcoming adversity. I was to learn that his early years in Spanish Harlem were simply a prelude to a story about how God's grace can change an individual, bring energy and healing into a life, and how one man could affect the lives of thousands of people.

Across the Christian Reformed Church and across Grand Rapids, where he did much of his ministry, Dante's story is unusual, his influence significant, and his life a startling example of what God can do with even the toughest of souls. He never won any big prizes nor held prominent positions. And yet his life, especially his barrier-breaking ministry in several arenas, is an example of how one man, remaining linked to who he was and where he came from, helped make racial, personal and even societal reconciliation evident in the lives and experiences of many people.

From my days as a *Grand Rapids Press* reporter and then from later interviews, I came to see that another of his unheralded accomplishments was in the neighborhood around Madison Square Church. When he arrived in 1978, the area was one of the most crime-ridden in the city. An air of desolation emanated from the streets and sagging buildings. Slowly, over time, by sitting for years on City committees and also by simply walking the area, talking to and ministering to the people, he helped in a process that in 2010 showed a transformed neighborhood.

Dante also has a wide-ranging legacy as a mentor to men and women now in ministry all over North America and beyond, in a range of denominations. His influence was powerful and wide. He touched untold numbers of people, helped transform lives, and did it all as a pastor who rose to his position from the hellish world of drug addiction and prison.

I met Dante at the Hospice facility. He showed me part of a short autobiography that he had written about his troubled youth. (Unattributed quotes in the text are taken from this autobiography.) He told me he wanted to write his entire story but feared time was getting short. Also, his concentration was not strong enough to get him through the rigors of writing a book. Although he looked tired and ill, he still had a spirit of well-being that attracted me. I wondered if we could meet for an interview or two. He was fine with that. As it turned out, he had gone to Hospice to get the pain from his illness under control. Feeling better, he wanted to go home. That is where we met. Sitting at a table in his basement, he told me his story.

Writing this book has been a wonderful journey. I have had the chance since to spend many hours with Dante's wife, Jackie Venegas. She provided much of the material for this book and helped me to see that, first and foremost, this is a story about using what might be considered liabilities and turning them into gifts. It is a story about perseverance by a man who accomplished what he did by offering his will and life over to the preservation and guidance of God. It is also a tale about a dramatic and lasting jailhouse conversion. In my research on Dante, I have come to see how God moves in the lives of people, and I have been able to experience some of the love and joy Dante had for his Lord.

Dante used his conversion wisely, becoming a minister whose work, especially his unerring compassion, touched and helped heal the lives of so many living in a community far from the streets and alleys of New York City and the bright lights of Broadway. He was a pioneer in his denomination, but that isn't what makes his story so unique. It was how God grabbed hold of this man and pushed him, through the power of the Holy Spirit, to perform a ministry that was truly special as described by many during his Memorial service.

I left there with a notebook full of information and a lump in my throat, thinking how it is clear that God was always there for Dante. He had taught so many that the same was true for them as well. He truly was one of the Lord's messengers.

Chris Meehan

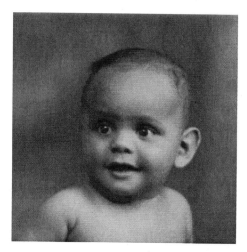

Dante Aligheri Venegas

Julio and Sara Venegas

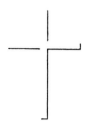

1
FAMILY HISTORY

The little boy was standing in the entryway to his apartment building on the corner of Madison Avenue and East 115th Street, just daydreaming, as he often did. He liked to simply look out at this small part of Spanish Harlem, watching the cars and people passing by. He enjoyed the sights and sounds and rhythms of the city. Maybe that was because, even at the age of four, he already had a poet's sensibilities. Things touched him deeply. His father, Julio Venegas, was a poet. In fact, his dad had named him Dante Alighieri Venegas after Dante Alighieri, the great 13th Century Italian poet whose most famous work was the *Divine Comedy*, which gave a detailed vision of Hell (*The Inferno*) and Heaven (*Paradiso*)—both places that young Dante would come to know as he grew, going through suffering and circling his way many times through Hell as he made his journey toward Heaven.

Although he looked African-American, Dante grew up in Spanish Harlem. His family was among the steady flow of Puerto Ricans leaving their homeland and moving into barrios in Spanish Harlem and in the South Bronx, hoping for a better life. They opened small *bodegas* and *botanicas,* hawked *piraguas* (flavored shaved ice) on the streets, and worked on the ship docks and in factories. For Dante's dad, it was also a place where bars and Latino social clubs were plentiful and where hungry ears for his poetry were always nearby on the bar stools.

Dante, even as a youth, loved all of the activity, much of it right outside his front door, which is why he was standing on the stoop at 54 E.115th Street that day in 1938. Most of the time, his mind flew free, chasing thoughts or just daydreaming, but not this day. Dante saw a small crowd of men, maybe 12 of them, gathered nearby at the intersection. They were all excited and clamoring around a central figure dressed in a white robe. The little boy wasn't sure what to make of it. He wondered if they were fighting or arguing. But then suddenly, the men fell back as the figure dressed in white began to slowly ascend. Truly, it was strange. This guy was rising into the sky. It was no magic trick, as far as Dante could figure. "I watched quietly as this figure slowly floated higher and higher until he disappeared into a cloud," Dante wrote in his incomplete autobiography. "I don't know if I knew Jesus at the time or what, but it was Jesus. And I saw Him go up and up and disappear in a cloud."

Dante was a child and then a man who had visions, many of them of God and heavenly things, but some of them of dark evil, of spirits that could destroy you with a whisper. He came from the Puerto Rican culture that was rich in expressions of the supernatural. So these visions, intermittent though they were, weren't unusual for a youth with his heritage. The boy watched the figure in white with amazement until it was consumed by the clouds. Even as young as he was, he knew what he had seen. He went inside and told his mother, Sara Hurtado Venegas, "I just saw *Papa Dios* (God)."

Many times in the following years, to friends on the streets, to fellow prisoners in jails, and then from the pulpits of churches, Dante talked about this incident. It was one of his first memories. The image was indelibly formed and firmly placed in his mind. In some ways, it shaped him and his eventual career—as one of the first Puerto Rican pastors in the Christian Reformed Church and a leader in breaking down racial barriers in that denomination and elsewhere. The image of that man in white stayed with him through many times, good and bad. "Even when I became a full-blown junkie (heroin addict), I thought of that man in white. He had to be God. Only God can do the things that have happened in my life. Only God gets the credit for what has happened to me!"

Dante spoke often about another memory. This one was also traced to his early childhood in Depression-era Spanish Harlem. But this was not a vision. Instead, it represented the harsh reality of what his early years were like. It, too, was a memory that seared his soul. He was home when a woman he didn't recognize came to the door and entered their apartment. His mother seemed to know her, if only in a formal way. Dante watched as that woman and his mother then disappeared into one of the bedrooms. He didn't recall if anyone else was around or what he had been doing. Out of curiosity, he walked over and peered through the keyhole. "What are they doing?" he wondered. "The woman was lying on her back as my mother stood in front of her, finagling shiny chrome instruments between the woman's legs."

That day, as he peered through the keyhole, he had no idea he was watching an illegal abortion. Even if he had, he wouldn't have judged his mother as being in the right or wrong, whether it was good or bad. Morality wasn't part of the picture. "I was a very quiet and pensive boy back then. That picture stayed in my memory bank with no judgment of it."

Dante never condemned his mother for a crime that took her more than once to prison. He learned, even as a child, that the world was a complex place. Making sense of good and evil, Dante would often say in his sermons, was hard. Both existed in his home, in almost equal doses, making him feel confused. Love mingled with anger and violence. God seemed to be in his home, "and yet, so was Satan."

Dante's mother was not alone in plying her trade. The key was in doing it safely. During the 1930s, as many as 2,500 women a year died in New York City from complications due to illegal abortions. Trained as a nurse, Sara Venegas was one of those who knew what she was doing, and the women she dealt with tended to fare well. Thus, many women sought her out. "I think my mother did abortions to maintain her family and our way of life as well as to obey my father. Deep down inside she felt it was wrong. She did it as employment," Dante said in an interview a couple of weeks before he died in 2007.

His mother was a prayerful woman and a longtime member of a Spanish Lutheran church. Being a devout Christian, the abortions tortured her conscience. Sara asked Dante once in the mid 1970s if he thought the Lord could forgive her for what she had done. "She knew where she was at with it. I told her that the Lord forgives everyone who repents. Look at what He did for me."

Forced largely by her husband to do abortions for income, Sara stopped doing them after he died in 1952. She then made a living working as a nurse at area hospitals. Dante always deeply loved his mother; she was so gentle, so kind, so loving, so humble. He noticed her devotion to God. She showed many times how important God was to her. He recalled how, when he was older, the cops came to the door one day to arrest him for stealing. After they busted open the door to the apartment, they looked around for evidence. Finally, they entered Sara's bedroom, where she was on her knees, never looking up, but continuing to pray for her wayward son. Having run past her room just before the police came in, Dante climbed out of a bathroom window and got away. All through her life, Sara continued praying for her son.

Looking back on those early days, Dante says, it seems like he was always drifting along, lost in a "dream-like world." He kept to himself, taking in the events around him. His dreaminess, his disconnection, may have been written into his genetic code and, he says, crazy as this might sound, could have gone back to before he was even born. There could be another reason why he felt so adrift in the world: He may have liked the warm womb of his mother so much that he didn't want to come out. Simple as that. He liked it there and wanted to stay. He was born one month after his mother's due date which made him wonder in later years if even *in utero* he may have sensed that things were not right in his family. He may have had the feeling that too much was going on out there, beyond the safety of his mother's womb. His mother's friend, Caridad, a midwife from Puerto Rico, delivered him on October 5, 1933 into a home already in turmoil. It was a home in which his father's dark, bombastic spirit prevailed.

"My father was a proud, loud Puerto Rican who drank whiskey. My godfather, Davila Semprit, may also have been there at the time of my birth. When I was born, my father, who was probably drinking at the time, exclaimed, 'El Gran Coco-Rocco'!" So, besides carrying the name of the famous Italian poet, they also called him "Coco," a name that stuck for most of his childhood.

Either way, it hardly mattered. He could just as well have been named "Ghost" for all he cared. He doesn't remember anyone paying much attention to him. He always seemed to be on the inside looking out. Maybe that's because his father always took center stage. "My father, God bless him, was a bright and gifted man, but he was an alcoholic," Dante said in his final sermon (*The Testimony*), preached in May of 2006 from the pulpit of Grace for the Nations Church in Grand Rapids. "My mother loved him, but she was also at the mercy of my father."

Dante, too, eventually found himself at the dark mercy of his dad who, once when driving his family while drunk, tried to crash them all into a tree. "Aha!" Julio yelled. "Now I've got you where I want you. See that tree up ahead? I'm going to kill all you bastards!" Frozen with terror, the family felt helpless when he stepped on the gas. But when a cousin in the back seat hit him in the head repeatedly with a shoe, he missed the tree.

Dante remembered his father frequently beating his mother. Dante and his sister would often have to pull him off from her, while also protecting each other from their father's blows.

Frustrated with the situation, he said, "Ma, let's leave this man. Come on, Ma! Let's go!"

"Son, I will not leave your father," Sara replied.

"Why not?" Dante asked, incredulous at his mother's response.

"Because I feel sorry for him," Sara answered softly.

Julio's cruelty extended beyond his family. Once, upon hearing from a friend in Puerto Rico that his wife was giving him a hard time, Julio got a bullwhip, flew to Puerto Rico, went to his friend's house and, when the wife answered the door, began whipping her. She escaped by running into the crowded street. Another time Julio got in an argument with his soon-to-be brother-in-law, going after the groom at his wedding with a butcher's knife. Fortunately, someone intervened.

The only time Dante remembered Julio showing any concern for him was when he discovered that Dante was using heroin. With a look of what passed for concern on his face, Julio gave him a bag of marijuana and told him to use that instead of the dope.

Dante's wife, Jackie, said, "With someone so volatile and cruel, Dante always felt on edge when his father was around." In many ways, the relationship with Julio was among the first circles of Hell that Dante had to confront.

Antonia, Julio B., Dante

Dressed in White

2
EARLY YEARS

The family members that Dante remembers coming to visit from his mother's side were his Uncle Samuel's daughters. They were a bit younger than Dante. On his father's side, there were visits from his grandmother, Antonia, whom they called "Mama Tonia." Julio's half-brother Piri and five teenage girl cousins would also visit. Julio's home became the transitional home for family migrating to New York City from Puerto Rico, a U.S. territory. They arrived by ship. All in all, it was a crazy place to live.

One cousin, Mayble Craig, lived for a time in the house when her family moved to New York City from Puerto Rico. She recalls the home as being chaotic and, at one point, an intoxicated Julio chasing the then four-year-old through the apartment with a steel pipe, bent on punishing her for something. Cousin Luis Venegas also remembers the home as chaotic when his family lived there. As a young boy, he would watch his father Luis Venegas in "Friday night fights" with Julio (his brother) in the kitchen, both of them very drunk. At times, the fights were brutal.

As long as Dante could remember, different people were always coming and going in his home. Feeling invisible, he moved among them, thinking that many of them were strange but also interesting. The people often stayed for a few days or longer. Along with family members in transit to a new world, there were poets, musicians and artists. Many of them, drawn there by his braggart/poet father who always attracted a crowd, were like shadows with no names. Much of the time was a blur, and the days blended.

But there was some stability in that his mother and his aunts—Titi Tili and Titi Rosa—were there for him to rely upon. "Tili was a few years younger than my mother, and Rosa was the youngest," he writes. Tili was married to a man named Pacheco, who one day died suddenly. Everyone was sad. Dante wasn't exactly sure why he died. But he did ride with his family to the cemetery to bury Pacheco. Other people were crying, but not Dante. He was interested in watching other people's emotions.

After they buried Pacheco, Dante started to skip back to the car. As he stepped over graves, he heard a voice that sounded distant and as if it came up at him from down deep in the ground. He heard his name, "Coco!" This startled him and he stopped, looking around and down, wondering who had called him. He didn't see anyone, though, and began running for the car. As soon as he got there, he reached his hand in the door-well and suddenly someone shut the door, trapping his hand.

He doesn't remember who slammed the car door on his hand. But it hurt terribly. He thinks they took him to a doctor. Other than that, he doesn't have much memory of the actual incident. All of his life, though, he carried a scar on his right ring finger from that time. All he had to do was look at that thin white line, and he could remember that voice calling "Coco" from down there in the ground, where all the dead people lived, and that door slamming tight on his hand.

Dante's mother often dressed him in white clothes as a young child. He is pictured proudly in suits, shirts, slacks and other white clothing in family photos taken over the years. Sara told him "many strangers thought I was a white baby." They told her he was a beautiful child. His baby picture, in fact, won an award in a New York newspaper contest, judging him as being the most beautiful baby of the year. He made his father so proud that he took Dante on a boat to Puerto Rico when he was only two years old to show him off to family members there. "Since I was the first boy child, it was probably a feather in his cap."

Dante didn't remember much about that trip. But he did remember how he felt. "I was on this freighter pulling away from the dock. I didn't want to be with *this man*!! There I was, watching my mother and my aunt waving goodbye as they gradually disappeared from my sight." Other than eating a meal of gooey white rice served up in an ice cream scoop on the merchant ship, he had no memories of being in his father's former home in Puerto Rico. He didn't remember meeting his grandmother, uncles, or cousins, or anybody. "It was as if I refused to relate to anything or anyone during the experience," he writes. "I was taken away from my world, and to me, no one was going to fill my heart with anything except those two women I left behind."

That was the first time his mother was taken from him. There were other times as well when she slipped silently away with no one explaining what happened, or why. "Everyone spoke in hushed tones and pained faces, but no one ever told me anything," Dante writes in his autobiography. "It remained a mystery." Later, though, he would learn that his mother kept getting arrested and put behind bars for doing abortions. His mother would disappear, and his Titi Tili would become his surrogate mother for long periods of time. Dante just went along with it. Ghosts don't ask questions. They just observe.

Other times he did more than observe. He had to participate. He had to drag himself from his dream world, usually because of something his father did or demanded. He recalls, he says, how Julio had him stand in front of a radio with a stick of spaghetti in his hand, commanding him to direct while classical music played. He also insisted that Dante play the violin and sent him to lessons. "All of this was always very painful to me. I would obey him, but never felt good about all his decisions for my young life." Dante didn't like playing the violin and would cry every time he played. Once, his father saw him practicing with tears running down his face, took the violin and smashed it over his head.

Dante's sister, Antonia, who was nicknamed "Papusa" and later called "Toni," was a year older, and she had a similar experience. Named after her father's mother, Antonia told him that their dad forced her to play the piano. She was practicing the piano when he got mad about something, blew up and slammed the piano lid down on her fingers. Experiences such as this led to Toni hating her father.

"Many of the experiences I had with my dad were quite powerful, of course; unfortunately they also shaped and gave bent to my future," writes Dante. "He was in my world and I had to deal with it one way or the other as a child." Dante often described his father as a misanthrope, one who hates mankind.

While never feeling genuine affection or caring from him, he did remember his father bragging all the time to others about how much Dante looked like him. Julio would wet his thumb and forefinger with his tongue and then would pinch Dante's nose as if to shape it. "I never said a word, but I distinctly remember the smell of spit and tobacco."

Dante's brother Julio was four years younger than he and was scared stiff of their father. Julio's facial features were full and lovely like his mother's, but he was named after their father. The name was a curse, and Dante's brother didn't like having it. But he didn't have to worry. He was born into a family who liked nicknames. His full name was Julio Bolivar Venegas; the family called him "Boli," short for Bolivar. "When Boli was a baby, I still remember playing with his beautiful soft baby feet. They felt good. He grew up with a temper like me. And like me, he hit the streets young. Boli was tough, but he feared my father like someone would fear God. He was afraid to laugh since my father would slap his head very hard if he did so."

The three siblings became very close as they bonded in protecting each other from their father's wrath. Dante especially tried to look out for Boli, walking him home from school, often boosting him on his back and carrying him home in bad weather. Each took a different way out from their turbulent home. Toni got married. Dante hit the streets and got hooked on drugs. Boli joined a gang and then the Navy.

Jackie says it is important to recognize the significance that being Puerto Rican played in Dante's life. While proud of his background, over the years he met many people who didn't know what it meant to be Puerto Rican, *Puertorriqueño*. Sometimes Dante would tell them that Puerto Rico is a Caribbean island situated a little over 1000 miles south of Miami. Puero Ricans have their own unique culture—music, food, mannerisms, customs and outlook on life. They are descendants from a combination of Taino Indian (original inhabitants), Spanish conquerors and the African slaves brought to the island. This has produced a very diversified population, a cultural and racial mix periodically described as truly multicultural. Dante's family typified this mix.

His grandfather, Estanislau Venegas, was very, very dark, very tall and very slim. He was a person with a fierce temperament, a strong persona, and a strong will. He was also very abusive. Dante's grandmother, Antonia, known as Mama Tonia, was from a large aristocratic Spanish family; she was white with long flowing hair. Estanislau was uneducated and worked as a carpenter; Antonia was a very refined woman who had attended finishing school, was artistic, loved to read and write as well as do needle work. Together they had five children, with Julio (Dante's father) being the oldest, born in 1900. "Unfortunately," says Jackie, "very little is known about Dante's mother Sara's family of origin. Their family name was Hurtado; there were 8 children in the family; her father was a traveling evangelist, going about Puerto Rico preaching; and one of her great-grandmothers was an African slave in Puerto Rico."

Always looming over Dante and the entire Venegas family in the U.S. was Julio and his explosive, violent personality. Everyone in the family feared him. Dante believed that his father transferred a mediocre spirit into him as a kid. He thought that was OK. He had made peace with the fact that he would never amount to much, that he would always be mediocre. Yet, a pulse of self-worth always beat in him and he kept moving forward, facing and transcending that mediocre spirit. In later years, especially as he had to preach before large crowds, he struggled to beat back these deep-seated feelings of mediocrity. But, say those who knew him best, the mediocrity never really won out. It simply tended to hide the magnificence of his nature.

3
SCHOOL DAYS

Dante loved his two aunts, Tili and Rosa. They were always close emotionally and geographically. They were never very far any time the Venegas family moved. Of the two aunts, his favorite was Tili. Since Dante's mother was in prison so much, Tili played a big role in raising him. But after Tili married Pacheco and got more involved in her own life, Rosa took over. And although she did it "*con cariño*," that is, with affection, she could be very hard on Dante and yelled at him a lot. Yet, behind the yelling was love. "I was somewhat awkward and always off somewhere daydreaming. If Rosa sent me to the store to buy eggs, you could bet that some of the eggs would come back broken, and me crying. I recall always bumping my forehead into doorknobs." Dante grew to respect and appreciate Rosa. He knew that, despite her gruffness, she cared deeply about him. She might scold him, but it was usually for a good reason.

So when his family moved from Spanish Harlem up to the Bronx, the person he missed most was Rosa. He would take the subway on weekends to spend time with her at 1776 Madison Avenue near E. 116th Street. Dante was about 11 years old at the time. "I remember the first time I went to spend the weekend with Rosa. I was walking past an empty lot spaced between two apartment buildings. It was one of those hot summer days and I walked, carrying an old army cot on my shoulders; in those days, the sleeping cots were made of wood and heavy canvass material. The stench of ghetto reached my nostrils, and I felt good. It smelled of home."

As a child, he went to kindergarten in Spanish Harlem. One of his first memories from that time is of standing in the classroom, needing to go to the bathroom, but not having any English to tell the teacher what he had to do. Feeling out of place, unsure of himself and the other kids, he started to cry. Tears flowed as his fear increased and the need to use the bathroom only grew. But he had a savior. The white teacher, Miss Ornsby, came up to him and somehow figured out what he had to do and led him to the washroom. He was able to calm down and pay attention in class after that, especially when it came to trying to learn English words.

Changes, however, always came fast and hard for him and his family. In the move to the South Bronx when he was 11 years old, he found himself in an all-black neighborhood. Given his dark skin color, he didn't really look different from the others. Even so, it was a tough adjustment to make. At that time, he was an innocent, knowing nothing about gangs or drugs. Again, Dante dazed along in his dream world. But that safe, self-absorbed place was fragile. It could last only so long. On the first day of school at P.S. 52 Bronx, a bully came up to him with some other kids around him; his name was Floyd. He was smooth, good looking, and had a sneaky, distrustful air about him.

He asked, "What's your name?"

Dante answered, "Coco." Ever since he was born, he had been known to everyone in his Spanish world as Coco.

But these guys didn't get it. They looked at him and one said, "Co . . . what?"

"Coco."

They looked at him like he was from another world, which in many ways he was, being from Spanish Harlem. The South Bronx was different and reflected the reality that Dante lived in a huge, mean city, a place in which children learned to fend for themselves or flounder.

One of the bullies asked, "Hey man! Where you from? Venezuela?"

Dante mumbled an answer.

Then Floyd asked Dante if he was wearing a pump.

"A what?"

"A pump, man! A pump!" he yelled.

Only later did Dante learn, he says in his autobiography, "that a pump was a mass of hair allowed to grow long in the front and it stood straight up; when it got real long you laid it back on your head with Murray's grease."

It was his first day of school, so naturally he was all dressed up, his hair greased back and shiny (but no pump) and wearing a green-and-white checkerboard-designed tie, which he thought was pretty cool. Looking at the tie, Floyd asked, "Where'd ya get that tie from, man?"

He had worn the tie because he liked it and thought he looked good in it. It made an impression, a hint of style he had gotten from his dad.

"Man, that's ugly," Floyd said. "Who you think you are?"

Floyd's words cut deep, making him feel a shame that he could not explain. All he knew was, it was only one of many humiliating experiences he had during those early days. They left an indelible mark on his psyche; it was very painful.

On another day, having noticed his accent, some kids surrounded him while one of them asked Dante to repeat the word "chicken."

He said, "Shicken."

They laughed.

Then the same kid commanded him to say "quarter."

In his Spanish accent, Dante replied, "Quorah."

They all roared in laughter. By this time, Dante says, he had already gotten the message: Either you identify and become as them, or you become the object of their ridicule. He chose to identify.

Although Dante's childhood was chaotic and painful, he still had some pleasant memories. One of his most precious memories was the effect of World War II on the people in New York. He recalled the brownouts, the air-raid siren drills, the way neighbors helped each other out, and the entire family gathering quietly around the big radio in the living room to listen to FDR give his famous fireside chats. He often said, "There was such a spirit of unity that felt wonderful. We were all in this together and looked out for each other. There was warmth among people." Enjoying a spirit of unity was something that stayed with him through all of his life.

Another good memory was of Halloween. They would take big socks, fill them with white flour and then go out into the streets and play a game where they would try and hit each other with the sock. The next morning the streets would be filled with white flour everywhere, not to mention themselves when they returned home. It was good, clean fun. There were trips to the beach and the country. They built and raced go-carts, and played in Central Park in Manhattan and Crotona Park in the Bronx. They played stickball and shot marbles. Dante liked to have fun, often joking in his bedroom at night with his brother Boli. He loved looking through his bedroom window and watching the snowflakes fall on the streets of New York City.

But Dante shied away from sports. He didn't take to the idea of being part of a game that required pads and helmets for protection; he wasn't keen on the idea of being bumped around, getting bruised and battered. Even when he tried to play baseball or basketball, he was just mediocre. "The other boys were the long-ball hitters, the high-rebound jumpers," he recalls. "I always felt unexceptional." It was a feeling he would battle all of his life. He always believed he fell short and hungered for more.

He never really followed any of the local teams and found himself left out of conversations about the Yankees, the Giants, the Mets and the Jets. In later years, he would get invited to Super Bowl parties and find himself enjoying the food much more than the guys bashing into one another on TV. He often wondered what his life would have been like if he had been able as a young man to talk the poetry that was really in his head, rather than try to talk about touchdowns and homeruns, to his friends. "Imagine me interrupting them in the middle of watching a touchdown pass—ball in midair—and asking, 'Have you read any of Garcia Lorca lately? Isn't he good?'"

Three Siblings

4
HOME

Dante's family did not have an easy existence, especially given the turbulence in his home. Poverty is hard, driving a family from one crisis to another. Rent was always due, and there was never enough money. How could they pay for the doctor when there was barely enough food to eat?

His family always lived on the edge, worried when they would have to move again. "Often you are at the mercy of landlords. You live in run-down properties; landlords make sloppy repairs if they make them at all," writes Dante in his autobiography. "When you are poor there can be a lack of educational attainment. You don't have the time or the focus necessary to pay attention to the teachers. You have to live every day in the survival mode. The emphasis in the home cannot be on education. Often parents are poorly educated and don't know how to get children involved and interested. There is a listless gap that can be filled with hatred for themselves and even at times for one another."

Dante's parents couldn't help him with his homework; that was the teacher's job. Anyhow, in his cramped apartment there was not a good place to stretch out with his books. Even if he had had the space, things were loud—lots of yelling, and people coming and going at all hours. No way could he focus, so he let his studies slide.

"I grew up with very little supervision. My father was virtually absent and my mother was always working. I think you know what happens when the parents are absent. You hit the streets. So I hit the streets at the age of 12." (*The Testimony*) He realized after a time that he liked the freedom of roughhousing outdoors, of getting dirty, of running down the alleys and dodging dumpsters, of dashing in and out of stores to steal candy or gum or to simply give people a hard time. On the streets, he felt unleashed, and he started to crave the freedom it helped him feel. "It was a fun life for me," he said.

As he remembered it, with the turmoil in his home and a father who often ignored him, the streets became his home and he started to see himself as just another plain old kid from "El Barrio." He learned what it took to fit in when they moved to the Bronx. In some ways, this experience of hanging around the African-American kids became one of his first introductions to "multiracial and cross-cultural differences." He knew deep down in himself that he had to deal with it, the difference. He could not tell his parents to move from 165th Street and Tinton Avenue in the South Bronx and return to 111th Street in Spanish Harlem. "I knew in my heart that I did not want to identify with Floyd, nor any of the other guys that hung around with him."

Some of the kids he knew organized into a street gang known as the "Slicksters." They were known to be tough and respected as gangs went. The gang close by in Dante's neighborhood was the "Copians," who also had a vicious identity, but not as bad as the Slicksters from 166th Street. Gangs were everywhere. You had to belong to a gang. But Dante wasn't interested in that, at least then. As he grew up on Tinton Avenue, the guys he hung out with just wanted to have fun, not fight. So by default they became a gang, called the "Happy Gents." They walked the streets laughing, talking about things other than fights. They took pride in being different. But they also got drawn into the drug scene.

Eventually, as the years rolled by, all the gangs were introduced to the new drug, at least in New York City, called Heroin. Getting high and loose on dope curtailed ambitions and brought on a stupefaction that meant gang violence in that part of New York City eased for a time. The drug was their magic potion. They didn't need to fight for turf. They could plunge that white mixture into their veins, and for a time, all strife between them would die away. Unfortunately, the solstice from gang warfare and violence didn't last. There was the issue of the demand outpacing the supply. Then there was the cost. Drug dealers sold it to you cheaply at first but then they kept upping the cost. "We all had drugs in common, and many of us died or were killed from one thing or another as I recall," writes Dante. "I had an alias back then; they called me Spanish Danny."

In *The Testimony*, Dante spoke about this time.

"When I began to use drugs, I didn't read the fine print, so to speak. The fine print said this: 'If you take this drug, you will be chased by the police constantly; you will be jailed time and time again. You will be sick, hungry and homeless. Sometimes you'll get high, other times you won't. Sometimes you'll get real dope; sometimes you won't. Sometimes you have to stick some people up and take their money, and sometimes others are going to stick you up and take your money.'

"I did not read the fine print. The devil said, 'Come on, join this club.' But it blinded me. I was blinded to the point where I loved drugs more than anything. All I wanted to do was shoot dope. But I didn't realize that the curse of the fine print was working."

At one point, he says, they were living in an apartment on Kelly Street, the street where Colin Powell, who would one day be a celebrated four-star general, was also living. Powell, a couple of years younger than Dante, attended the same schools Dante did. While Dante's family didn't know the Powell's, they did know one West Indian family, the Thomas's, who had two pretty daughters. The older one was Claire, and the younger one was Winifred. Claire attended Morris High School with Dante. "We were in the same grade. She was a sassy, quick-witted, foul-mouthed chick who held her own and was very popular in school. Everyone knew and liked her. She always had a bunch of girls hanging around her," writes Dante.

One day, Claire "hit on me in front of some of my friends while we were yukking it up in front of the school at the close of the last class period."

Dante and a friend were standing at the top of the stairs, and Claire was standing at the lower end of the stairs with some of her girlfriends. The friend punched Dante lightly and pointed towards Claire. "She's talking to you, D, and she's trying to get your attention."

Dante said, "Hey, whassup?"

She yelled back, above the din of the crowded school steps in a confrontational voice, "How come you don't talk to girls?"

Dante felt the challenge, typical of Claire, and took it. He got to know her and they became good friends. That meant he got to hang out in her parents' apartment above their candy store with Claire and the rest of the girls once or twice a week.

"I thought that was one of the coolest things I had going on in high school, hanging out in a large room with all those females, just having good old fun, talking and laughing," he writes.

Dante remembers flunking out of Morris High School because he would inject himself with heroin and come high to American History class, his last requirement to graduate. He would slip into his "junkie nod" and sleep through class. He was strung out, unable to do the work. Heroin dominated his life.

For a time, it was the answer to the chaos generated by his father at home. Dante began to see that he could run from those things that confused and troubled and stifled him. Like a dog let loose in a field, all he did was run. Literally. He ran to hustle up the money to buy drugs. "I ran to find 'a pusher' who had the drug. I ran from the detectives who knew me by name and by sight. I ran from dudes whom I had cheated out of drugs or money; run, run, run."

All of the running wasn't bad. Dante says he simply liked to run, to race through the busy streets of the neighborhoods he knew. Running made him feel free. He loved how it made his lungs burn and yet seemed to heighten his senses.

One day he was running past an empty lot. He was living in the Bronx at the time. Something made him suddenly stop running and look at the debris strewn in the lot. There was nothing special about this lot. It was just one of many in the ghetto. For some reason, though, his eyes singled out a green stalk growing through all the junk in the yard. "It snatched my attention as if it were speaking directly to me. It was an odd scene, this brazen young stalk of green, growing out of a sea of junk."

He was young. But even in the broken pieces of concrete and bricks, the abandoned kitchen appliances, the twisted pieces of metal, the broken glass and empty bottles, he saw in that lone stalk of green, life at work—a life in some ways that was way beyond how he was then living.

Thinking back, that stalk could have been his burning bush. Maybe it was God poking through the soil. He had no words at the time to express how that green stalk made him feel, but it stayed on his mind and eventually, he came to see that it represented life, creation, and the creator God. It represented this thing, this impulse that was sprouting inside of him. It reflected the presence of that God whom he once saw float high, high into the sky above that bevy of men. It hinted at his future, rising through the junk, looking for the sun. But he didn't stare at the stalk very long. He just kept running, trying to tear loose from a life at home that confused and frightened him. His mother would be there for a time, and then gone. White men in long coats would knock on the door and, if she was there, take her away. Dante remembers one time that, when word came down the street that the police were on their way, he frantically helped bury Sara's medical instruments in the ground, hoping she wouldn't be arrested.

5
"POP"

While Dante deeply loved his mother, it was his father who, in many ways, shaped him. It took Dante years to understand and come to terms with his father. Healing began with realizing that his father didn't have it easy as a kid.

Dante's father was born in Puerto Rico in 1900, but he left when he was about 16 years old. Julio Venegas wanted to escape. He hated Puerto Rico, and he especially hated his father, Estanislau, who had abandoned his wife and their five children to go live with another woman. Julio didn't even want to talk to his father. They were sworn enemies. Julio held no kind sentiments, and instead nourished a boiling anger toward the brutal man who left their home and failed to provide for his children.

However, one time, says Dante, Julio asked his sister Carmen Maria if she would go to their father's house and ask for fifty cents so Julio could buy some tennis shoes. He needed the shoes so he could get a job on a merchant ship that was leaving Puerto Rico. Barefoot teens were not allowed to work. As the story goes, Dante's grandfather told his daughter, "You tell that SOB that he is just as much a man as I am; let him get his own money the best way he can."

Hearing that, Julio told Carmen, "I'm leaving this god-forsaken place. I can't stand to breathe the same air this man is breathing." Somehow, he got a pair of shoes and made it onto that boat before it left for Panama City. As for Dante's grandfather, he lived his life in Puerto Rico and died of a heart attack one day after walking a long way to Carmen's home, seeking forgiveness and telling her he was sorry for how he had treated the family.

Julio was known for making profound or flowery statements. As the oldest child, he was intelligent and gifted as a poet. But he was also hot-headed and single-minded. Once the ship docked, he lived in Panama for about two years. After Panama, Julio sailed to Italy, where he fathered a child named Gina, studied poetry, became fluent in Italian and took on the airs of an intellectual. Dante didn't know much about his father's seven-year passage in Italy. But he did meet Gina. "I saw Gina once when she was visiting her mother who lived on a farm in Canaan, Connecticut," writes Dante. "Our entire family drove to Canaan from New York City."

The experience stuck with him. They drove out of the crowded city, along roads lined with tall trees and through quaint New England towns. Once they arrived at the farm, Dante saw a cow for the first time. The animal was wandering the farm field when they arrived. Dante stared, watching it move slowly along, bending to eat grass, oblivious that it was being watched by a little boy from Spanish Harlem. But there was something else. "I remember being told there was a bull shut up in a little red barn down the hill near the crystal clear creek. I remember feeling a bit apprehensive about that bull." He didn't like the mental image of a big bull bursting through its barn and thundering across the field, nostrils flaring, to knock him over.

So he turned and went up to see his family and to meet Gina. But, despite worry over that bull, he kept thinking of the creek, the ever-flowing water. At some point, he left and, as if drawn to a new world, walked down to the creek whose water was so clear and cold, it appeared drinkable. They didn't have creeks like this back in Spanish Harlem. Watching it flow, he took off his shoes. He wanted to explore the new surroundings. It was like a fairyland to him. He recalls wondering where that stream went, maybe the ocean, and feeling a kind of fluid happiness pour into him. He wondered if this is what it was like in Italy: happy and free and clear. Pure, even. He would have to ask Gina.

He decided to check it out, to wade in the water. It was cold and bracing, but he didn't get out. He had a problem, however. Without his shoes, his feet had a hard time with the small rocks that he hadn't seen before. "I was impressed when I waded into the ankle-deep water, but it ran over and around too many golf and tennis-ball-sized rocks." He was far away from Harlem, and part of him loved it. It was so different from anything he knew.

That was a fun trip, so unlike the painful family trips to Bedford Hills, in upstate New York, to see Dante's mother. Sara was incarcerated in the Bedford Correctional Facility for Women, a maximum security prison, for performing illegal abortions. Julio added to her misery by getting into arguments with Tili and Rosa over whose turn it was to visit her, at times resulting in no one making the trip. He would write letters to Sara, complaining about her sisters and the children. He never showed concern for her or took any responsibility for his role in putting her behind bars.

For many years Dante was haunted by thoughts and memories of his dad. He recalled his father asking him to play catch with him one day. Julio was a star pitcher for the *Cuban All Stars*, a semi-pro baseball team at the time. He handed his son a mitt and told him to get into a catcher's crouch, which Dante did, staring out at his father as he started his wind up. Dante remembers watching his father's graceful movement and loving the fact that his dad wanted to play catch with him. He was happy. But then his dad pitched the ball. "As the ball came towards me, I was poised to catch it; but suddenly it curved away from my mitt. I never understood that. The memory stayed in my heart for many years. My father threw me a curve ball! It missed my catcher's mitt completely."

Dante knew little about baseball during those days. Even so, his father took him often to his ball games. Julio would seat his son way out in the outfield and give Dante the job of holding onto his wallet that was forever stuffed with wads of cash. "I just sat there quietly, watching him pitch. I thought he was a lousy pitcher because he threw so many pitches that the batters couldn't hit. I didn't know then what the object of pitching was."

His father would take him to bars around the neighborhood where they lived in the South Bronx. He recalls one time going with his father to an all-black bar. As they walked in, the attention immediately went to his dad. People turned and called out, "Julio's here!" His father sat Dante at the bar and then said, "All the drinks are on me." Everyone cheered. They were happy Julio was buying. This happened a lot. "Pop used to just throw money away. I got used to it and began sitting close to him when he got drunk. Each time the bartender would bring the change from a hundred or a fifty-dollar bill, I would siphon off most of it and slip it into my pocket. When he got really drunk, one of the men would help him home. As soon as I could, I would give Mom all the money I had siphoned off from the bar table."

It seemed like everything his father said was hilarious to the men drinking at the bar. He was good with words. One time someone asked Julio if Dante was his son. His dad quickly replied, "I don't know, but the little SOB is always calling me 'Pop'." The entire bar roared with laughter for, what seemed to Dante, an agonizing two minutes.

Sometimes, his father returned home from the bar with his entourage at three or four in the morning and called for his wife, whom he called "Pata," to cook for everyone. "Pata, make some *arroz con gandules y bistec*," Julio would bellow. Dante's mother would do it. One time Julio asked for rice and beans.

After tasting them, he asked angrily, "Did these beans come from a can?" When Sara nodded "Yes," Julio grabbed the pot and threw it out the window.

"My father was always 'center stage,'" writes Dante. "He was a very charismatic man. As long as I could remember, there were always different people in my home. Either they lived with us for a while, or they were part of the entourage that always followed my braggart father. Our house was like Grand Central Station. I never knew what I would wake up to in the morning. We had visitors from Europe at times; we had celebrated musicians who were popular in the Latin world; we had baseball players, boxers, you name it. They all would come to Julio's house on Tinton Avenue in the Bronx."

"My father was a strange bird," Dante said. "When he was sober, he was a great guy. He dressed very well, was very intelligent and likeable. But when he drank, he was crazy. Pop was a poet. He had a gift of oratory that was mesmerizing. When his friends would come to our home, he would recite from the poems he had written. I heard them so much I could have committed them to memory without trying very hard." Julio was a member of the Poet's Society and spent a lot of time with this group.

In 1970, Sara, Dante and Jackie were invited to a reunion of the Poet's Society. Sara didn't want to go, but Dante encouraged her to do so. When they arrived, Sara was treated like a queen. Dante really enjoyed talking with the men who had been a part of his life so many years earlier. It was obvious that Julio was highly regarded by this group, many of whom had led productive lives. They gave a wonderful tribute to him and his leadership of the group. In some ways, it seemed a bit surreal to those whose lives had been negatively impacted by Julio. And yet, in another way, it was like salve being put on an open wound.

Dante remembered being eight or nine and his father taking him along in the car. He parked the car, left Dante alone in it, and went up the stairs to an apartment. Dante recalled the shades of the room where his father went were pulled. Shadows of his father and some woman were in action behind it. Dante never said anything to his mother, Sara, about this experience, but always associated it with the birth awhile later of Plinio Ruiz, Dante's half-brother. He wasn't sure how he knew about Plinio, but he saw him a couple of times when he was a kid. Since Plinio lived with his own mother, Dante didn't get to know him until the mid 1990s when they re-connected and built a strong friendship.

Blasphemous to the core, Julio wasn't a churchgoer; but Sara was. She had, in fact, grown up in the home of a traveling evangelist. Sara made Dante go to learn Catechism at the nearby Spanish Lutheran church that she attended.

Not happy with going to church, he asked his mother, "How long do I got to do this?"

"Until you make your Confirmation."

"And then what?" Dante asked.

His mom wasn't exactly sure, but she said, "You can do whatever you want after you make your Confirmation."

Recalling this conversation many years later, Dante said: "So I made my Confirmation. I learned the Apostle's Creed; I learned the Ten Commandments and a couple of other things. And I knew there was an Old Testament and a New Testament. Then I left that church when I made my Confirmation."

Some time later, he went back, sat in a pew and stared at the preacher. He had 25 sticks of pot in his pocket. The preacher was talking about sin. At some point, he shook his fist at Dante, as if he knew that the young man in the pew, the kid who made his Confirmation there, had lots of pot in his pocket. Dante sat there, feeling guilty, knowing that the preacher was talking right to him. "It felt like those marijuana sticks were burning up in my pocket," Dante recalled. Soon, he got up, went to a party and didn't return to that Lutheran church for a long time. Even when he returned, though, the experience would not be good.

Dante's Father, Julio

Dante, Toni and Plino Ruiz

6
FRIENDS

Dante had many friends, but there were two men who reflected different aspects of his personality. One was a friend; the other a bad role model. The friend was named James Boldon. He lived a block away from Dante's family and was not the type of guy Dante usually wanted to hang out with. James was kind of dopey and awkward and overly serious. "But he was a nice guy, a couple years older than me and very intelligent. James, an African American, was intent on learning to speak Spanish. The only Spanish family close by was ours," he writes. James would come to the house almost daily. He had no vices and was very square in Dante's estimation. He even walked weird. He took long strides and rocked from side to side.

Yet, something attracted Dante to James, a Roman Catholic who attended Mass regularly. They talked and hung out a bit. Dante saw something steady and curious in the other boy's personality and outlook on life that he found attractive. Catholicism was this strange, far-off religion, a faith that taught a salvation Dante was sure had to be unattainable for him.

There was this other thing, too, that both repelled and brought him a little closer to James, who would often sit for hours at Julio's feet whenever he was reciting poetry. "I was amazed at his ability in memorizing my father's poetry and reproducing it on paper. He actually spoke and wrote Spanish better than I did." He even visited Puerto Rico once and met Dante's relatives.

Dante never totally understood this relationship. "I always considered him a friend even though our worlds were vastly different. As the years went by, we lost touch with one another. When I saw him again, he was involved with a popular Afro-Cuban occult religion, *Santeria.*"

At one point in Dante's search for some meaning to life, he had been involved with this same religion, a religion with many gods. He was attracted especially by the intense, elemental rhythms of the Bata drums and the unhindered dancing during services. He loved playing the drums. He even was asked by the *Santeria* priest to take up the intense study required so that he could perform in certain special rituals as well as in the ordinary ones. But he held back, fearful of where it might lead him. In this religion, spirits ran rampant, summoned up by the drumming. Dante wasn't sure how they could be best understood and contained.

One night, however, proved to be too much for him. He was at a *Santeria* ceremonial site in someone's home, the standard meeting place for the secret rituals. "I was really into my drumming when, all of a sudden, a live goat appeared in the apartment." Animal sacrifices were an integral part of only the special rituals. "I was shocked. Sacrificing an animal in a New York City apartment?! I didn't know why, but inside I felt very uncomfortable: 'Something's not right with this!' As soon as possible afterwards, I split from the scene."

Then there was Sonny, who was smooth, polished, snorted cocaine and smoked reefers. Dante was 13 or 14 when he met Sonny. He was drawn to Sonny and his lifestyle. Sonny was the "numbers man," a hustler. He was cool and slick and not serious like James. He moved easily in and out of places in the South Bronx and Harlem, selling and buying drugs, taking numbers, paying off the gamblers when necessary, but mostly collecting. "I was so impressed with Sonny that I wanted to be like him when I grew up. He was a role model for me in those early years living in the Bronx," writes Dante.

Try as he might, though, Dante could never pull it off 100 percent. Sonny had a hard, unreachable quality that, mimic him as he tried, Dante could never quite attain. His conscience was always at work and he had a sense that he could, should lead a better life. "I could talk the talk, but not walk the walk," he said. Out of loneliness and a bent toward self-destruction, with really nothing going on in his life, Dante turned to the path Sonny walked and began feeding his veins with heroin. In 1950, by the age of 16, Dante had become a "junkie," a full-blown heroin addict.

From there, he started to get into real trouble. He was arrested in 1953 by federal agents and charged with altering his draft card for an older guy named Babs, who used it for an ID to cash a stolen income tax check. When Babs got caught, the police determined the identity of who truly owned and had altered the draft card. They arrested Dante and he ended up being sent for one year and a day to the U.S. Public Health Service at Lexington, Kentucky. This was a minimum security prison/ hospital where the government sent drug addicts like Dante, then 19, to prison while also attempting to bring about a cure. There was a department where monkeys were used for research. They would addict a monkey to "smack" (heroin) and then observe as the monkey went through the withdrawal process, trying to learn how they could help cure addicts.

During his first incarceration—for altering the draft card, a charge called Aiding and Abetting—he tried to stay to himself and steer clear of trouble. Even so, during this first time behind bars, he began in earnest to learn the criminal's trade, being taught things that kept sending him to prison for years to come. "When you go to prison, you go there to learn; you don't learn the good things; you learn the bad things," Dante said in his final sermon. Things like learning how to steal checks from locked mailboxes in apartment buildings, forge his signature on them, perform con games, become a really good pickpocket, sell drugs and do stick ups.

But he also had perplexing, thought-provoking experiences behind bars. Dante especially remembers one of the federal agents yelling to him at that time. "Look at you! You're a good-looking kid destroying your life with drugs. I know what I'd do if you were my son."

The agent's remark got him thinking. Just as lost in booze and drugs as his father was, he often wondered how his life would have evolved had Julio ever expressed the emotional concern the agent had. "I was just a dumb kid who tried to block out psychological pain with heroin. My mother was in prison, serving three years for doing illegal abortions, and my father was a pitiful drunk living in a great big house on Tinton Avenue. It was sad thinking of him existing without my mom: lost, 'fallen,' and drinking cheap booze."

The home that had once pulsated with people from all walks of life had now become a flophouse. Everyone in his family was displaced. When he wasn't behind bars, Dante recalls being homeless and sleeping on roofs of tenement buildings before homelessness was something mentioned regularly on the news.

As for Julio, when he realized in 1952 that he was dying while in Lincoln Hospital in the Bronx, he called the Governor of Puerto Rico, a childhood friend, telling him, "I refuse to die in this god-forsaken country." Gov. Luis Muñoz Marin sent a plane to fly Julio back to Puerto Rico where he died at age 52. "My father died from cirrhosis of the liver. While alive, he had money, friends, fame and prestige. Yet in the end, he died alone, having lost it all and lost his family—hopelessly addicted to alcohol," Dante wrote. Julio's half-brother Piri took charge of the burial; Sara reimbursed him with a money order sent from prison.

In September 1964, Dante wrote, "In my 19th year (1953), soon after my father's death, I lay half-wake, half-sleep in a still and quiet room—incarcerated for the first time. And my father woke me with a familiar slap to the back of my head as he swung and hollered, 'Dante!'"

7
GOD WAS WATCHING

After his release from Lexington, Dante came out clean. But it didn't take long for him to return to his habit, moving into his early 20s in a hazy, drug-induced stupor, hardly aware of himself, more often than not thinking he was no good and destined for worse. Being hooked on heroin, he needed money and did what it took to feed his habit. "I just kept running as usual, until the law would finally catch up with me and imprison me for my yearly hiatus," he writes in his autobiography.

Looking back as he approached death, Dante said: "I believe God always had His hand on me even though I never knew it. He was always speaking to me in ways I did not discern." Dante recalled stories that even years later made him laugh and shake his head. God was there; he just wasn't paying attention. He remembers one time hanging out in a Third Avenue bar in the Bronx, drinking and getting high, already having popped some pills, waiting for something to happen. Maybe a lucrative opportunity would come his way. By chance, a truck driver was sitting at the bar having a drink.

A guy everyone called One-eyed Cy quietly came into the bar, slipped next to Dante and informed him that the truck belonging to the man drinking at the bar was unlocked and full of meat. Just there, said One-eyed Cy, for the taking. "We both left the bar and opened the rear truck door; and sure enough, it was full of meat. The only problem was that it was 'hanging meat.' Huge parts of cut-up cows hung on hooks."

Flabbergasted, Dante looked at all of that meat and told One-eyed Cy to climb in the freezing trailer and start sliding the meat off the racks. Dante said he'd stand below, stacking them as they came out, at the same time keeping an eye out for police or the truck driver. He wasn't quite sure what they would do with all this meat.

Suddenly, quicker than he was ready for, One-eyed Cy pushed one of those frozen carcass parts out and onto Dante's shoulder, making him stagger. "I don't know what I was thinking, but that piece of meat was almost as tall as me. I hoisted the meat on my shoulder," he said.

High from the beer and drugs, Dante decided to flee with the frozen hunk of cow, wondering as he ran where he could stash it. As he was running across the street, someone yelled, "Ride 'em, cowboy!" The idea came to him to drop it off inside one of the nearby tenement lobbies or hallways. He could wait awhile and go back and get it if nothing happened. Just then, though, he glanced up and saw a very bright full moon. "I don't know why, but it was one of those moments in which I believe the Lord was speaking to me. It was as if He were saying: 'I see you.'"

Dante couldn't explain it—only that it was a transcendent moment, an instant when he felt pierced by what he later came to believe was God's presence extending itself to him. It was as if God was reminding him that He had his eye on him. As for the meat, Dante didn't say what he did with it. It was the otherworldly experience that mattered.

Another time arose when he believed the Lord was trying to communicate with him. He was riding the 3rd Avenue El from Harlem to the upper Bronx, where he was living at the time. He was so high on drugs and barbiturates that he could barely see. It was about 3 a.m. when he staggered off the train, down the stairs, and started walking home. "I looked up at the sky on one of those chilly, cold, star-studded nights; the stars were twinkling bright like diamonds. Again, it was as if God spoke to me through my drug stupor. He said 'I'm still here, I am Eternity, and I don't change.'" Again, he felt that piercing, a sense of God trying to get his attention.

But the thought of God slipped quickly away, lost in the abyss into which he was falling. Bleary-eyed, he stopped in front of a bargain clothing store. There were no bars protecting the windows. He peered inside and saw the cash box. Looking around, he found a metal milk crate, which he hurled through the window to break the glass. "I went straight to the cash register and opened it, only to find rolls of pennies in it. I was so angry and disappointed that I scooped up two armfuls of children's blue jeans in various sizes," he writes. "I believe that even a dumb cop could have busted me. All he had to do was follow the trail of jeans I periodically dropped as I stumbled all the way home." The next day he arranged all the jeans he had not dropped into appropriate sizes, bagged them, and went back to the ghetto community to sell them to mothers with children.

Not all of his experiences were of drugs and crime. Dante had a vast appreciation for the city itself. He loved the soaring buildings, the traffic on the streets, and the vast mixture of people. And then there were the city noises.

Dante recalls a balmy April morning in the 1950s. He was simply resting on his bed, near an open window, and heard "the stirrings of another day." He heard the Madison Avenue bus rumble away from the corner stop. His ears followed the sound as it shifted gears and rode away. Once the bus noise diminished, he heard the bang and crash of garbage can tops. A garbage truck was out there filling itself with refuse. Then he heard a fire engine screaming its way to answer a call. There were the blasts of car horns, pedestrians passing by and talking, and the sound of metal security grates being raised as businesses opened. He loved it. The sounds filled him with energy, even a kind of happiness. Noise to the city dweller, he says, is part of the daily routine.

Watching the passing scene in NYC, years later

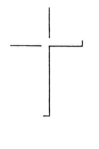

8
BEHIND BARS

Despite his yearning for a better life, Dante would be jailed many times over the years, but ending up in the Raymond Street Jail in Brooklyn for his first arrest by the New York City Police Department—it was 1955—was an experience he would find hard to forget. He was arrested for shoplifting. Before then, he had kicked his heroin habit for the first time at the federal public health facility in Lexington, Kentucky. Here he had another chance to get off the heroin. That he did. But he also, during this time behind bars, picked up many more tricks that would help him once he got out and continued his use of drugs and his life of crime. He would be in other jails over the years. But it was the first one that stuck in his mind; it was when he started to see himself, and to think, as a criminal. This is when going to jail, doing time, became a lifestyle.

During this time, he was going with a nineteen-year-old girl named Reva. He was 21. What he remembered acutely is that he received a letter from her that was nine pages long. Shaking it out, it didn't contain a much-needed money order, which he had hoped for so he could have spending money. This made the other inmates laugh. They made fun of him and told him that he should write Reva back and tell her that he wasn't a goat, that he couldn't eat the letter, especially one that long. He ignored the taunts and recalled looking at that letter. It was dated, May 5, 1955. For some unknown reason that date was impressed into his mind as a significant one he would remember as long as he lived: 5/5/55. The number five had always been a favored number for him; it could be that he was born on the 5th day of October. He didn't know, but being involved then with Numerology, he tended to see repeated numbers as omens, good and bad. This one seemed bad.

The walls of his cell at Raymond Street were made of thick plaster, and they seeped water from the dank humidity. Dante was locked-up for 23 hours every day and then provided a 45-minute walk in a small outside walled area. The prisoners could not stop walking on that exercise break. They had to keep moving.

Raymond Street was like a Bastille from the old days, the jail in France that the people stormed in July 1789, sparking the French Revolution. Dante used to tell people that this jail must have been built around the time the revolutionaries took over the Bastille and made away with its cache of weapons. Raymond Street was large, cavernous, wet and very, very old. There was a captain in charge of a shift named Walsh. He had huge hands and appeared to be in his sixties. It was rumored that he had beaten and killed inmates with his shovel-sized hands. Whether this was true or not, Dante didn't know, but he believed it. Dante avoided him whenever he could.

In a way, with his newly developing convict mentality, Dante was impressed with the reality of being in such a tough jail. He enjoyed all of the rough talk from the guards and hearing his cell-block gate slamming shut as someone called out the warning: "On the gate, South 8." He recalled clearly the feeling that overcame him when he heard that command and terminology, followed by the loud banging of the closing gate. It made him feel proud and tough.

Being locked up seemed almost pleasant to Dante. Now he really had become one of the bad boys from the streets. "It was as if I were entering into an exciting world of jail and prison heretofore unknown." He learned how to carry himself, how to defend himself and how to steer clear of the cons that were big trouble. But feeling proud about being a prisoner didn't last. "Little did I know then, that I would eventually tire of this brave new world, for fear that it could very well be the destiny for the rest of my life."

9
DOING TIME

About two months later, Dante was released from Raymond Street, but it wasn't long before he was in trouble again. He returned to the drug scene and all of the hassle involved with supporting a heroin habit. He began putting into practice what he had learned. Unfortunately, he writes, he never became the smooth crook he wanted to be. The closest he ever came to being the sophisticated criminal of his imagination was when he was stealing and forging checks, known on the streets as hanging paper. He discovered that he was good at it; hanging paper was his favorite and most profitable vocation. Besides, "Paperhangers were somebody in the community."

"I was twenty-one years old and crazy. I didn't care about anything but when my next fix of heroin was coming. I believe the reason I enjoyed hanging paper so much was that it took a fair amount of skill in spotting and slipping a check out of a mailbox without having to break the lock. I didn't want to break the lock because, if I got arrested for stealing checks out of a mailbox, they would tack on an additional charge of destroying government property if the lock was broken."

Hanging paper allowed him to exercise some of his in-born ability. He may have considered himself mediocre in most things, but he sure could talk. "You have the gift of gab," his mother told him.

With this gift, he easily convinced clerks and storeowners that indeed it was his name on the check he was trying to cash. Fast-talk alone, however, wouldn't do it. He also learned and came to enjoy erasing and falsifying names on a phony ID he would present with the pilfered check. Late into the night, he bent over a desk and worked hard to mimic the signatures of other people. It was meticulous, exacting work that demanded great focus. He loved it.

In 1957, the FBI arrested Dante for hanging paper. Charged with Uttering and Publishing, he was sent to Lewisburg Federal Penitentiary in Pennsylvania, where he did three years from 1957 to 1960.

In Lewisburg—home to lots of lifers, Mafia members, murderers and even spies—Dante got a job carrying steel to make lockers, but that job was dangerous and cut up his hands. When he saw guys on an upper tier working in an interesting-looking space, he decided to check it out and found that it was the tailor shop. Dante asked for a transfer and started working there. His new job entailed sewing clothes, and in the process, his wily convict's mind discovered a secret place in the waistband of his pants to stash his drugs. Once he was released from the penitentiary, he tried it out often, daring the cops to pat him down. They never discovered the secret pouch.

He met a guy named Joe Maitland there. He liked Joe, who had a good sense of humor and had a sense of rightness about him. He was not a tough guy, but commanded respect from everyone by the way he carried himself. "We had a good relationship between us," Dante says, "even though he was five years older than me. Joe was an excellent check thief. I admired anyone who acted professionally in his learned craft."

Then there was a guy from the Bronx named Frank, who could very easily pass for white. He had blue eyes and was very fair-skinned. His father was very dark, and his mother was white. Dante and hard-hearted Frank would later pull many armed robberies together while in Brooklyn. At first, they used a butcher knife, until Dante got hold of an old, broken-down .32-caliber revolver. In retrospect, he says, it was comical. The revolver's barrel had been sawed down, made to look just like a Detective Special; but whoever sawed it down cut it crooked, and it just looked plain cheap. "We only had three bullets, and the chamber that held the bullets wouldn't revolve when fired," he says. Nonetheless, it looked intimidating enough to get the job done.

Dante learned to do prison time successfully, not by marking X's on a calendar each day, but by seeking inmates whose interests in jazz, the arts, humor and, at times, the occult made everything else in the "punishing prison" tolerable and invisible, if non-existent. Here he also met a streetwise preacher who would have a great influence on his life.

Dante used to say, according to Jackie, that he "hung around with the poets, the comedians, and the musicians. They would laugh and laugh and talk about music, poetry and art. This was how they would do their time." These friends helped unleash his creativity and he would write poems and stories and draw pictures and cartoons in a notebook that he always carried with him in a pocket.

However, Dante always had to be on guard. Trouble and violence could break out at any minute. One time, he learned that he was the target of an intended rape. Not about to let this happen, he stole a fork from the kitchen and fashioned it into a shank. "When the would-be rapist started to make his move," he said, "I made it very clear by emoting intense feelings of 'threatening and slaughter' that I was not going to let that guy have his way." Dante didn't even have to resort to his shank to protect himself. His words and his angry, hardcore attitude convinced the guy that Dante was not a man to mess with.

Despite the continual threats in prison, Dante met many memorable characters during the years he spent going in and out of penal institutions from 1953–1965. One of them was a guy called Calcutta. One day he startled his fellow prisoners by suddenly walking around and yelling, "I've got the key! I've got the key! I found it! I found it!"

"The key? What kind of key?" the guys were wondering. Calcutta wouldn't answer. Wanting to know, the guys began speculating among themselves whether he might somehow be able to set them free.

"What do you mean?" they shouted when he began yelling again.

"When we are out in the yard, follow me." Following instructions, they excitedly gathered around him. When he had their attention, he yelled in a drawn-out manner, "The key is lo-o-o-v-e!"

"The guys were more than angry with Calcutta," Dante recalled.

Then there were Pie Face, the con man; Raymond, the schizophrenic; Subway, the lovable but insane genius who quoted Shakespeare; and Chink and Chatty, two Harlem gangsters with an "off the hook" sense of humor which led Dante to believe they really were crazy. They were "clowns" who mocked anyone and everything in prison; perhaps that was the way they chose to do their time—just pretend they were nuts.

"Playing crazy may have been how they did their time," Dante writes, "but they really didn't have to work too hard at pretending." Some time after being released from the prison he shared with them, Dante ran into Chatty on 116th Street in Harlem. The gangster invited him up to someone's apartment. Before sitting down, Chatty removed a huge long-barreled pistol from his belt and set it on top of the coffee table. "I really believe Chatty was 'nuts' and people were afraid of him because of it. In prison, there were inmates who were recognized and labeled 'fools.' You never knew what such men were capable of doing. With fools, you never made eye contact, simply because of their unpredictable behavior."

10
"AM I WORTH SOMETHING?"

At one point in his travels through the criminal justice system, Dante had a very unexpected, even transformative, encounter with "Piggy." Piggy was one of his high school friends who moved with the rest of the group into the drug scene; he was a good-looking African American man with a great sense of humor. Joe Jenkins was his real name.

Piggy would always be smiling and chuckling when he spoke. Dante liked him a lot and committed petty crimes now and then with him in order to get drug money. A few years after high school, they ran into each other in jail; Dante couldn't remember the exact time. They talked and reminisced. One day much later on, Piggy stopped by to see Dante as he was writing a poem inspired by "Black Rose," a woman he was involved with. This would be a turning point of sorts. This is when Piggy, of all people, would recognize something in Dante that he failed to see in himself.

Explaining Black Rose, the subject of the poem Piggy saw, Dante said: "She was one of those proud African American women with an attitude. She wore a beautifully sculpted Afro, complimented by a beautifully sculpted body that caused women to envy and all men to drool. I would often go into a controlled rage whenever Black Rose and I would go out on a date."

"Black Rose was crazy in love with me. She would do anything for me. We had a very interesting relationship. She and I would smoke weed together and drink a little wine once in awhile, but she never used drugs, nor prostituted herself to earn a living."

Deeply attracted to her, he was never quite sure how to act. She lived in two worlds—the one he inhabited and the straight (non-drug/crime) world, which is maybe why she confused him so much and he had to write poems about her. He never stole anything from her, nor did he ever ask her for any money for drugs. Dante could never quite understand their relationship.

But back to Piggy, who sidled up and asked what he was writing.

"Just a poem," said Dante. "I always write."

Piggy asked if he could read it, and Dante showed it to him.

"What are you going to do with it?" Piggy asked after looking it over, obviously impressed.

"Toss it in the trash like I always do."

Then Piggy asked a question that really made Dante think. It turned on a light within him.

"Do you mind if I keep it?" asked Piggy.

Dante wondered if he was kidding. But he wasn't.

"No, man, you can have it," Dante replied.

He was surprised over Piggy's reaction since he firmly believed that anything he produced or did wasn't worth much to anyone. He watched Piggy actually reading it again and seeming to enjoy his words. It made him wonder that, if his buddy Piggy thought it was good enough to read and to keep, maybe the poem was worth something to someone. Maybe, for that matter, he was worth something to someone, or at least there was that possibility.

Sometime later, Subway, the Shakespeare quoter, did the same thing. Dante tossed a poem in a trash container and Subway went after it, telling Dante he really could write.

Black Rose, for that matter, would always encourage him to write. She was already involved in the world of arts and entertainment through a modeling agency she had started and would often ask him to write up articles for some of her brochures, announcements or advertisements.

Many of their friends thought he and Black Rose, a black woman with piercing eyes and flowing hair, were going to eventually be married. Dante says he never thought so, and they never did. He could never quite make the push it would have taken to be with her permanently. At first, he figured it was because of him and his mediocrity. Still, he wrote her longing love letters when he was in prison. Only later did he realize that it would be his total belief in Jesus that would divide them.

11
SPIRITUAL REALITY

After serving three years in Lewisburg Penitentiary, Dante was released. Free of heroin and his criminal skills honed to a fine point in what many called "The Big House," Dante hit the streets of New York City and soon was strung out. Once again, he "boosted" from stores, worked on perfecting his pickpocket skills, sold drugs, and stuck up liquor stores with his buddy Frank and that useless, botched-up gun. Even as he kept up with the criminal life, something nagged deep inside of him. A sense of uselessness and a hopelessness he couldn't explain away dogged him, eating at his mind, gnawing at his heart.

One day during this time, Dante found himself leaning on a railing overlooking the East River. He had been walking along and had felt compelled to stop. He looked into those iron-gray river waters. It was a day on which he felt especially bad. A black despondency hung on him, clasping him in a depressing grip. His world felt blocked, dead-ended, worth nothing. He wanted to die. After a time, he remembers calling out in desperation: "Godzilla, if you will come out of the river right now I will follow you!" Somehow, yelling these words helped to break the hold that the dark cloud had on him. He almost smiled, imagining a big monster's head emerging, dripping water and bellowing an answer to the request, asking Dante to follow him, back into the water, down into some deep places.

Dante wanted answers. Bottled up and confused, he was also angry and at his wits' end. If someone had made this cock-eyed universe, then Dante wanted him or her or it to show their face so they could talk. But nothing happened. Godzilla, the Japanese film monster that menaced the world, did not drag his ugly head out of the water. No beam of light struck Dante down. No whispering angels alighted on his head. He was still left with himself, the flowing water and that terrible black hole only the dope could fill. He remembers raging at the water, at the sky, at the sprawling city, desperately seeking answers and direction. He felt so alone and lost. Not even Godzilla was around to help.

Yet, there were many well-intentioned people who cared for him and wanted to see him delivered from the life he lived. One was his Uncle Samuel, a spiritualist who was Sara's older brother. The news had reached Puerto Rico that Sara's oldest son "Coco" had turned into a drug addict, and they were devastated by the news. He had always been such a nice boy, they said. How could this happen? Hearing about Dante's troubles, Uncle Samuel sent Sara a small amulet. It was a silver-looking hand with a slit of red in the palm, representing the bleeding stigmata hand of Christ. It was enclosed in a triangular-shaped plastic case with a short beaded chain at the top, making it possible to be used as a key chain adornment.

Uncle Samuel advised Sara to tell her son to keep it on him at all times because it would deliver him from all harm. Dante always carried it with him. Every time he was arrested and commanded to empty his pockets, this Christ amulet would always be part of his belongings. Since he was frequently getting arrested, especially on drug charges between 1960–64, the good luck charm apparently did not keep him from "all harm," as intended. But it did start him thinking more seriously about Jesus on the cross and the death He suffered for everyone, including Dante, through the offering of his body and blood.

Dante wrote many years later that maybe it did do its "mystical work," since Jesus did eventually command his undivided attention, reminding him in a powerful way that the spiritual world is real, irrespective of what anyone else says or sees. The amulet and that hand with a nail hole through it became important to him, pointing to a new beginning. "My uncle in Puerto Rico may have actually seen my future salvation."

Another man, Serge, a spiritualist in New York, apparently saw the grace of God in Dante and gave him the Yoruban, West African name Imi Yemi, which meant "in the grace of god." Dante liked that, but he couldn't quite accept it. He still felt desperate and in need of direction.

Seeking answers that wouldn't come, at one point Dante consulted an astrologist. Dante himself was deep into astrology at this time. The astrologist told him to never wear black caps unless they were lined with white. Dante followed the advice, thinking that oftentimes actions that appear to have no meaning can be used by God for intended good. These, of course, were strange tidings, and yet Dante was always searching, grasping for something solid that held meaning—a meaning he sensed, but never quite felt, in that church where he was confirmed many years before and where the pastor later pointed out the young man with weed in his pocket.

Even in the worst of times, spiritual reality was and remained a part of Dante's life. Visions and a profound, if misguided, sense of holiness were part of it, starting when as a youth he saw the figure of Christ rising into the clouds, to the time he heard someone calling out his name from a grave. Then there was the time he was stealing meat and saw the huge, star-studded sky. Or the time he spotted that one stalk of green poking out of the ground in that slum lot. God was there, and the spiritual world did exist, even if it kept coming and going, approaching and then slipping from his grasp.

Later, though, this would make sense and he was able to explain it: God never moved from Dante. Instead, he was the one moving away from God's grasp. "The grace of God operates whether we believe it or not. Joseph told his brothers, 'You intended to harm me, but God intended it for good to accomplish what is now being done, the saving of many lives,'" wrote Dante years later, quoting Genesis 50:20 (NIV).

Dante was not able to pay much attention to Scripture in his days as an addict. Yet, there were those who saw his struggle and reached out, even when he would refuse the help. Despite the sorrow and guilt and confusion he felt in these years, he eventually realized that a sustaining seed had been planted in him in the late 1950s by a man named Herbert Daughtry. The seed slowly but surely took hold, eventually blooming in a most unexpected way.

12
NOT READY YET

When Dante first met Herbert Daughtry in Lewisburg Penitentiary in 1957, Dante told him that he was acting cool on the outside, but inside he was having a difficult time adjusting to prison. He was trying to get into doing his time, but things kept bothering him. Daughtry's answer was puzzling. He said: "You have to get ahold of something that will lift you above these prison walls."

Daughtry was to become the pastor of his father's Pentecostal church not long after this meeting. At the time, though, he was behind bars. He immediately took to Dante and saw in him a longing that Daughtry himself had felt and had found out how to fill. Dante also took a quick liking to Daughtry as well and saw an honesty in him that was lacking in many other prisoners. The day after talking to Dante about doing time, Daughtry gave him a Bible and said, "You need to get into this." He taught Dante a lot, especially how to fill his days with thoughts of things other than himself. It's funny, though, says Dante, how one learns from people and experiences without ever really thinking, or saying to yourself, "I'm learning." He spent time with Daughtry and part of the man rubbed off. They were to feel a kinship that would last through the decades until Dante's death.

Rev. Daughtry was an impressive man, says Dante. Although he was doing time, he was a Christian unlike any Dante had ever met before. Daughtry was a regular guy. He didn't smoke cigarettes, he played a real good game of basketball, and he cleaned up on the pool table. In fact, he loved and could play sports. He would one day become a chaplain for the New York Jets football team. Dante also admired his brain. Daughtry was one of the most intelligent men Dante had ever met. He had an unusually keen mind, and memorized large portions of Scripture that he interspersed in conversation whenever he and Dante talked.

Hailing from Brooklyn, Daughtry got into trouble growing up despite his religious rearing. His father was the Bishop of the House of the Lord Pentecostal Church that had been founded in Georgia and had started other churches across the south before moving north. Daughtry told Dante that the congregation was waiting for him, Daughtry, to come home and take over the church. His father had passed away during his incarceration. Rev. Daughtry was a man of many talents. He would go on to found the National Black United Front and serve as a leader of the African Peoples Christian Organization. He would travel the world and speak to many audiences, and get into knockdown, drag-out struggles with the politicians of New York City. Even behind bars with Dante, he showed that he had the personality of a leader and a mind that could grasp big ideas and memorize speeches. "The one thing that impressed me most was the July 4th speech of Frederick Douglass that he committed to memory," recalls Dante.

Rev. Daughtry was very politically active in civil rights causes, but he also remained a dedicated and committed Christian brother who "practiced what he preached." He may have had harsh opinions, but he walked in holiness.

When Daughtry's out-date at Lewisburg came before Dante's, he asked Dante, "When is your birthday?"

"October 5th, why?" said Dante. He was born in 1933.

"I'm going to send you a birthday card while I'm out there."

Dante said to himself, "Yeah, right, I'm sure you will." He had heard those promises before from good-intentioned inmates who never made good on them. Daughtry, however, lived up to his word. Their friendship really began when Daughtry sent the card. When Dante left Lewisburg in 1960, they kept in touch by telephone. But Dante was strung out on dope again and had no intention of attending House of the Lord Church.

He did keep the letters, though, sent to him by Rev. Daughtry. In one, the Pentecostal preacher wrote, "There is so much you can do with your life, so many constructive things that you can accomplish, and it is really a shame and a pity to destroy it with dope." In the same letter, he said, "I will write you again soon or will see you soon. I will be praying for you constantly, and you pray, too."

In another letter, Rev. Daughtry listed the things Dante needed to do in order to be saved by God and then to lead a Christian life. He wrote: "Put away sins, and don't compromise with any known wrongs. Quit them . . . resolve now in your heart that with the help of God you will not do them. Also, break with your former associates who are still doing wrong." Dante read this letter over and over because of the sound advice it offered. In it, Rev. Daughtry also told Dante to pray often. "Set aside two times a day for prayer, preferably first thing in the morning and last thing at night; and pray as often during the day as you feel led."

Rev. Daughtry also advised him to study the Bible by reading at least four chapters a day. This way he could read through the Bible in a year. In addition, he recommended that Dante memorize at least one verse per day and copy down passages that spoke to him. Daughtry told him to pay especially close attention to the Gospel of John.

There was more. Rev. Daughtry told him that he must be a worker, a witness, for God. "Tell someone else what God has done for you." He then wrote a sentence that Dante held onto all of his life, especially after he entered the ministry. "Remember that most people—however they appear outwardly—are confused, tormented, restless, guilt-laden, spiritually sick, mentally or emotionally disturbed or socially maladjusted." By knowing this, Dante could look beyond the surface and, with compassion, try to "be the instrument which God wants to use to bring them to Himself."

Finally, he told Dante to remember always that he needed to ask God in prayer to show him how to act and to regularly ask God to let him know the plan that the Lord had for him. "Strive then," wrote Daughtry, "to lay a good foundation, a strong foundation."

These words hit home in many ways. But even as Dante drifted, Daughtry continued to stay in touch. "I'm glad he did; he was the only one I knew who explained some of the things that happened to me," said Dante. One of these was the inscrutable working of the Holy Spirit.

But soon he forgot, or shoved aside, what Daughtry taught him. Dante wasn't ready yet for the Lord. He kept taking drugs and was forever getting into trouble. Later in life, when he was off the streets as a junkie, he came across a Bible passage, which he wished he had heeded earlier: "Be not drunk with wine, wherein is excess; but be filled with the Spirit." (Eph. 5:18, KJV) Sorely lacking contact with the Holy Spirit, he kept looking for relief and release in drugs. His life had become so miserable, so full of despair, so driven with attempts to figure out the perplexing aspects of life that he often became frantic, sensing the flames of Hell—of Dante's inferno—licking at his heels. Relief only came with another shot of heroin.

One day Dante copped some dope in Harlem and wanted to "take off" as soon as he could. Feeling sick, he couldn't afford to wait until he got back home or to duck into some alley. So he grabbed a cup of water from a luncheonette and climbed five flights of stairs to the roof of a tenement building on 116th

Street. Up there, he unwrapped his "works" (drug paraphernalia), cooked the drug and shot up. The drug roared into his bloodstream, hitting him fast and hard. Soon his blood flowed with a wonderful, heart-slamming warmth, filling him with fleeting ecstasy. He loved that stuff. Feeling fixed on the inside, he started back down the stairs. They were dark and his mood started to plunge. He was in the habit of carrying a notebook and pen with him. Reaching a lit landing, he sat on a step and wrote this poem. It was about his drug habit, termed by junkies as the "monkey on my back."

MONKEY, WHY?

In a stupefied, mystified,
  Unjustified lie,
And gathering the pains and
  Weariness of long lost souls;
I ask, opified, bleary-eyed,
  Ostracized, why?

Surely something's been
  Done that may be undone.
And I ask, and no answers yet;
  And—why?

Sitting on the step, his heroin high starting to falter, he wrote on, the words tumbling out, as he asked questions of that monkey on his back.

Searching in dimly-lit cellars
  For answers too bright to
Be found there, but I do, and ask
  Myself, why?

Children ask why, and those
  Wise enough.
I am not a child
  Nor as yet wise enough.

Still, I search falteringly,
  I search doubtingly,
  I search hungrily,
  In a long sad, Why?

"I used to wonder what would have happened if I had channeled all my junkie energy into pursuing a formal education instead of a fix," Dante wrote years after scribbling that poem in the staircase of the tenement. "Perhaps I could have made it in the field of advertising since I had so many creative ideas running through my head continuously. I had the habit of cartooning and drawing pictures with captions that spoke a million words; at least I thought so."

By now, Dante had extended his life as a hustler to three boroughs of New York City: the Bronx, Brooklyn, and Manhattan. Queens, a middle class haven, wasn't worth the trip. He says he always wanted to be a sophisticated crook. The cons taught him to be a smart crook, not a show off. They also taught him, although he didn't follow their advice, to steer clear of violent crime. At one point, seeing the men dressed in fancy clothes and the women who worked for them in skimpier clothes, he decided he also wanted to be a pimp. He tried it, but didn't really have the heart for that type of crime.

In *The Silent Sound of Needles*, author Michael Zwerin chronicles the life of drug addicts like Dante in New York City during the late 1950s and the 1960s, writing of how terribly restless and how horribly hooked the addicts really were. The dope came from Southeast Asia and was strong and relentlessly attractive. This was the period just before the flower-child era of the late 1960s, when drugs got a stranglehold on the United States. Few people had used heroin until this time. Dante told Zwerin that he often felt remorse about his drug use and talked to God, pleading for divine help in getting him clean. He went into rehabs, had those stints in jails and prisons, would go straight for a time, but always went back to the needle. Even so, he kept searching for God, maintaining a slim connection that would eventually turn him in a different direction.

During this time, Dante moved from one single-room apartment to another in different boroughs, trying to stay ahead of the police and keep from getting arrested. Much of his life seemed hopeless, and yet there were times when he tried to do the right thing. One day he turned a corner in the Bronx and suddenly came across a guy who had been shot and was bleeding to death in front of the bar on 170th Street and 3rd Ave. The guy's head was resting in a sewer grate. Dante rushed to him and held his head off the grate, getting bloody himself, watching as the man's life ebbed. The man's eyes reached Dante's, his head bent to one side, eyes rolling back, and Dante's heart went out to him. He was well aware that he could have been that dying man many times. The blood that stained his clothes could have been his own. When word came down the street that the cops were on their way, Dante knew he better vanish so as not to get involved. He feared being accused of the murder. So he gently set the man's head back down, careful to keep it free of the grate, and disappeared.

Then there was another, although much different, sewer grate story. One cold winter night Dante found himself in Brooklyn, desperate for money to purchase some heroin. He made the decision to stick up a cashier at the Loew's Kameo movie theater on Nostrand Avenue and Eastern Parkway. He recalled being shocked by the woman's terrified screams, thinking that since he had no intention of hurting her, why was she so terrified? He slowly walked away from the scene so as not to draw attention to himself, threw the gun in a sewer grate farther down the street, and continued on his way.

For a short time during this period of his life, Dante came into possession of a master key that fit all General Motors cars from 1950 to 1960. He wasn't interested in using the cars for transportation. Rather, the key allowed him entry into those automobiles without calling attention to himself. The items he stole from them and then sold on the streets would bring in much-needed money for drugs. During an arrest, the police officers discovered the key hidden in one of his pockets and confiscated it.

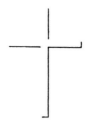

13
"I'M NOT GUILTY!"

By 1964, Dante at 30 years of age had grown weary and profoundly distressed over his drug use. On January 1, 1964 he wrote: "I can't do this anymore. I don't feel it. There's no soul attached to it! 'Let me go, Devil!'" Try as he might, he couldn't kick it for good. Drugs were his friend and mortal enemy at the same time. He was sick of being put in jail or prison. He was worn to the bone by the everyday hassle of "dodging narcotic detectives, security undercover cops in stores, drug addicts whose hustle was sticking up pushers selling dope in the notorious block of 117th Street in Harlem, etc. Everything was old."

The streets were mean, with danger constantly lurking everywhere. Crime of all kinds, a white powder that could either be pure heroin or be laced with a deadly substance, the threat of overdosing, always looking for a means to obtain the drug—all of these controlled Dante's existence. At any moment, his life could be snuffed out.

It was hard for him to remember if at one time he thought the life he was living had been going somewhere. He remembered standing in front of a bar on Third Avenue in the Bronx one day with a dope-fiend friend called Snipes. It was rumored that Snipes had murdered someone. Dante felt awkward standing there in the cold with his hands jammed in his pants pockets, waiting, he had no idea for what. But something told him that he needed to be elsewhere. He turned to Snipes and said, "Hey man, I don't belong out here, do I?"

Snipes surprised him by an emphatically drawn out answer, "Helllllll No!"

After leaving Snipes, Dante started to think he had become so desperate and had lost so much hope that no earthly thing, no hospital, no rehab center was ever going to deliver him from the bondages of heroin addiction. "I was starting to believe it would have to be something supernatural to deliver me from my bondage." Early in 1964 he wrote: "Why aren't you dead?" "Because I am waiting for life, Fool! These years I have spent on earth in ignorance are but a preparation for the good that is to come to me. When it comes, it shall be for the good, for I already know evil, and I do not wish to know more."

Many years later, Dante preached: "I didn't know God. I was into astrology, philosophies, *espiritismo*. I knew all that stuff. People wanted to give me a washing to cleanse me and then get a fish and honey. I said, 'I don't want all that!' It seemed like God did not want me involved with anything. He had something reserved for me that I didn't know about. God said, 'I am the one who is going to save and deliver you, and no one else. Only God, only Me, only I will get the credit for what I am going to do for you.'" (*The Testimony*)

One night, alone in his rented room in Mr. Wilson's house on W. 122nd Street in Harlem, he got down on his knees and prayed, "To Whom It May Concern: Stop me from using drugs." One tear dropped to the floor. He waited, listening. He paid attention, checked inside his heart, kept his ears tuned to sounds. No answer came. Dante wasn't upset. He could understand why some higher power wouldn't answer his prayer. After all, he was such a sinner who had no real faith.

Then his mind turned to someone who had real faith, his mom. In the midst of all the madness, his mother was a strong Christian, and he knew she was fervently praying for his deliverance. "Why doesn't God answer her?" he asked. "All her prayers and all the people in Puerto Rico praying for me, and I'm out here strung out on dope? There can't be a God!" All he felt was a helpless void inside of himself.

Convinced that prayer wasn't going to work, he got off his knees and went to bed. Not long after, he got up, left his room and took the subway up to the Bronx. It was very early in the morning of May 2, 1964. He had a five-dollar bill in his pocket, enough to buy a small bag of dope if he wanted. But he was determined to stop using drugs. Drugs still attracted him. Getting high held a nasty allure. Still, he wanted to stop. He needed to stop. Maybe God wasn't going to help; maybe there was no God who cared for him. But he had to quit the dope.

It wasn't long before he was tested. He ran into an old dope-fiend friend whom he knew and liked. The friend was selling wine to anyone who wanted to drink after the bars closed at 3 a.m. He asked Dante if he knew where to cop some dope at that time of the morning. "I told him that I indeed knew a connection, but added that I had just kicked a habit in Manhattan General and wasn't interested in using any dope. He practically begged me to get it for him," said Dante. "So I drank some of the wine and got loose."

Together, they went and bought the drugs. On their way back, they stopped in a small corner grocery store to buy some potato chips. "Thirty seconds after leaving the store, I heard a voice command us to lift our hands up into the air, turn around and go back to where we came from."

A cop named Carnegie, sitting in the back of the store, came after them and marched them back to the store. The grocer pointed at them: "Lock those two men up! They stuck me up three years ago!"

Dante laughed. The guy couldn't be serious. He had been locked up for so many things he had done, that he just knew this had to be a hoax—definitely a case of mistaken identity. He had never robbed this guy. "I don't know you! I've never seen you before in my life!" But Dante, in a moment of sudden, cold clarity, knew that might not matter.

He feared what might come down on him, because, he said, "I didn't do that robbery. I wasn't guilty. Still, I was facing 40 years if convicted." He remembers, for some reason, that at the time of his arrest he had in his pocket a well-read copy of Aldous Huxley's *Time Must Have a Stop*, a mystical novel whose protagonist Sebastian asks many of the very same questions that Dante had been asking about the meaning of life, about whether there was an unseen world beyond the one that he started to fear wanted to put him in jail again. The cop took the two men away and booked them on charges of armed robbery.

While he hadn't stuck up the store, Dante still was technically hooked on heroin. So the guard at Bronx County Jail, where they took him and numbered him Inmate #264-3762, marched Dante to a holding cell on the fourth floor—the floor where they kept all the dope fiends, and a floor that he had visited many times before. As the guard led him through the gate and onto the tier, a guy named Drake, who was in the very first cell, asked, "What they got you for, D?"

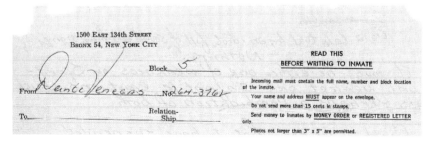

Dante turned to Drake, a guy he knew from hanging around spots on Longwood Avenue, and replied, "Armed robbery, but I didn't do it."

Then someone else in one of the cells called out, "Who's that comin' in, Drake?"

"It's Spanish Danny."

"What's he busted for?"

"He said armed robbery, but he didn't do it."

Laughter erupted in the cells and someone else said, "I didn't do it either." Then another person yelled, "We're all innocent in here."

The laughter made Dante mad. In retrospect, though, he wouldn't have believed it if someone like him had come in, protesting his innocence. Even his mother, who visited two days after his arrest, didn't believe him. He told her he didn't do it. The grocery store owner had to mean someone else had robbed the place. Sara Venegas listened quietly and nodded her head, saying, "Yes, son, I know." But the look on her face betrayed her; he knew she thought he was making it up.

While they talked, he recalled the African American astrologist who had seen two children in his chart and had told Dante never to wear a black cap unless it was lined with white. With his mother across from him, it suddenly dawned on him that, on the night he was arrested for the bogus armed robbery, he had been wearing a black cap with no white lining. Weird as it was, he wondered about the significance of it and asked his mother to consult a woman named Lillian, *la espiritista*, a spiritualist to whom his family often turned for advice. He wanted his mother to ask her why he was being charged for an armed robbery he didn't commit.

Sara followed up. Lillian looked into her spirit world, telling Sara "no one could have prevented the arrest because it was orchestrated and pre-ordained by God Almighty Himself." When he heard this from his mother, Dante wondered if it was true, if God cared enough to send him to jail. Or was it the evil spirits he had been courting through his drug use that put him behind bars? He knew that sometimes for the addict there was a thin line between good and evil, between God and the devil. Maybe Lillian had it right; maybe not. He had no solid ground to stand on. No God to whom he could plead his predicament.

Or so he thought. Little did he know how much the ground was about to move. What happened was like an earthquake.

Bronx County Jail

14
"TO WHOM IT MAY CONCERN"

In jail once again, Dante felt worthless. He felt weak and useless, a rag thrown into some gutter. He was at the bottom of a deep hole he had dug for himself. "I began to think that prison was the lot the gods had prescribed for me," he said. He had been trying to get help and had started calling out, not sure if God—or was it Godzilla?—heard him or even cared.

But then, and he had a hard time explaining it, even in his wretchedness something surprising and miraculous happened one night soon after he arrived. For a moment, he thought of Lillian and her world of spirits and how she had said the arrest was in God's plan. Hard as it was to believe, he felt a hand reach down in the muck and mire in which he was living. He felt a pull on him in that cell, and then a tug and he began to think, "Baby, I better hold on!"

Significantly, that night in his jail cell, the change, a full transformation, finally began to happen. It was **May 5, 1964**. Broken and bereft, Dante fell on his knees and cried out "To Whom It May Concern."

"'Well, God, **if** you're God, there are two people who know I did not commit this robbery: You and me. However, there are some other things I've done.' And I began to recite and recount all the sins I had committed and all the wrongs I had done to people. Now you know this is the Holy Ghost moving because I didn't know anything about confession. I didn't know anything about forgiveness. I didn't know anything about God. Then I said,

Bronx County Jail Cell

'If you can forgive me for what I did, I would appreciate it. But if you can't, I understand and I forgive you.' That's when the dance began!!

"It felt like dirty sheets were coming out of me. I didn't understand what was going on. I've been in homes where people didn't change sheets, and I know what dirty sheets look like. It felt like they were just being pulled out of me, pulled out of me, pulled out of me, pulled out of me, pulled out of me until I was exhausted. Then I climbed up onto the top bunk.

"In the morning when I woke up, I went to jump off the bunk—and I floated off the bunk! I said, 'Uh-oh, uh-oh.' I felt something go '*Ummmm, Ummmm.*' I felt mellow. I felt all clean inside. I felt like honey was in there. I said, 'Whooaa, whooaa.' I felt like I was a candidate for Bellevue. 'I've gone nuts. Something's wrong here! I'm high without smoking anything!'

"So then I said, 'Ohhh, ohhh. This has got to be from God!' Are you hip to the 'Lucky Dip'? There was a New Testament over the cell. Thank God for the Gideons! I picked up that little King James New Testament and I did the lucky dip. I said, 'Lord, this has got to be from You!' I rolled my fingers over the pages. Bam! And it landed on Romans 13:10.'

> "Love worketh no ill to his neighbor; therefore love is the fulfilling of the law. And that, knowing the time, that now it is high time to awake out of sleep: for now is our salvation nearer than when we believed. The night is far spent, the day is at hand: let us therefore cast off the works of darkness, and let us put on the armour of light. Let us walk honestly, as in the day; not in rioting and drunkenness, not in chambering and wantonness, not in strife and envying. But put ye on the Lord Jesus Christ, and make no provision for the flesh, to fulfill the lusts thereof.'

"Was God speaking to me?! He was speaking to me through the steel bars and concrete of a guarded prison. God broke through those prison walls and took Spanish Danny—and turned him completely around!" (*The Testimony*)

Dante heard what he thought were pigeons flapping their wings and flying away. He came to believe later that those weren't pigeons at all. He understood them to be angels rejoicing over one sinner who had repented.

When he was younger, his mother sent him to that Lutheran church where he made Confirmation at the age of 13. But that didn't save him. The little hand of Christ in a plastic case didn't save him; the many promises to God or "To Whom It May Concern" that he was not going to "do it again" didn't save him. No, this was not about a teenage ceremony, a lucky charm, or prayers uttered from the gaping, drug-ridden foxhole that was his life. It hit him: Salvation had been there all along, a gift freely available to all. The Bible passage confirmed it.

So there he was, facing 40 years for armed robbery, and for some reason he felt good. Something had grabbed hold and gone deep. Scales fell from his eyes, mind and heart. He told God that he would gladly be willing to serve 40 years behind bars if He would grant Dante the honor and privilege of serving the time with Him and be in His glory.

"Hallelujah! I was saved and knew it! I did not understand why I suddenly began to comprehend more fully what previously was unintelligible. I read the Bible. I didn't understand why I felt so much pity and compassion for the addicts who were arrested and sent to my floor to kick their drug habit," Dante wrote.

He realized he wanted to help them, especially in that terrible period after they had gone through the four or five days it takes to kick a heroin habit. After the pain and misery are over, Dante said, a phenomenon occurs. Since they had not eaten anything while kicking their habit, junkies get "the chucks." After vomiting everything, even green bile, and then settling down, one could eat enormous amounts of food and still not be satisfied. Dante recalls an inmate junkie, experiencing "the chucks," putting an entire loaf of bread on his tray already piled high with food. An officer asked if he was planning to eat all that food. The inmate looked puzzled and said "unh-huh." The officer warned, "If you do not finish every bit of food on this tray, I will send you to the hole." The officer watched this hungry junkie slowly eat every single morsel of food on his plate. He didn't get stuck in the hole.

"After lock in, I would hear the guys in the cells complain and wish they had something to eat. I would take whatever I had—Hershey bars, Snickers, Milky Ways, etc.—and slide it to the man in the cell next to me and whisper instructions to run it to the hungry man, but not reveal the source it came from," he said.

Enthralled and driven by his newfound faith, he would purchase extra commissary items for the sole reason of freely giving to the men who "had the chucks." He didn't understand why he did this, but simply felt a need to do so. In a letter from that jail, Dante wrote his friend Rev. Daughtry and said that he found himself quoting the Bible, talking to his fellow inmates about the love of God. Instead of rejecting him, the other inmates listened. He spoke their language. He was not some outside chaplain. He was one of them. He even started taking a group of inmates to Protestant services on Saturday night in the jail. "You know, Herb, in your last letter you mentioned the indwelling Christ-like Spirit, and in your letter before that, you said God has plans for me," Dante wrote. "And I have to smile sometimes, 'cause I want to do so much that I'm afraid of losing the Christ within me. It's so new and beautiful that I want to walk with Christ every day."

Dante spent three months in Bronx County Jail, going back and forth to court. During this time, he told himself that he was not going to plead guilty to an armed robbery he had not committed. On the one hand, Dante felt that there was little justice for minorities in the United States Court System and that the symbol of a blindfolded woman holding evenly weighted scales in her hand was hypocrisy. If he left his life up to the judge, he would lose it. On the other hand, he felt a definite daily presence of God with him. God was doing and telling him many wondrous things. Sanctification was happening inside of him. "I truly believed that pleading guilty to something I did not do was a grievous lie before Him," said Dante. "It was as if a truth mechanism had been planted inside me."

He was experiencing God's power in amazing ways. The music pumped through the speaker directly in front of his cell was, of course, secular. It was doo-wop and be-bop and raunchy, restless rock n' roll. But God was doing an incredible thing with the music he had to listen to. Each song he heard was automatically transformed into a song of grace and love for Jesus. He couldn't understand why this was, but he didn't fight it. He swam with it, bathed in a joy he had never known.

The intense feelings of compassion, caring and providing for others were also manifested in prayers. Dante had a cell mate for a short time who told him about a wine-drinking dude who hung out with junkies. He was obviously out of his element by hanging out with dope fiends, even though he did not use heroin. "As my cell mate was telling me the man's story, I felt intense pity for the man and was led to pray for him and his family," Dante says.

Another day, while standing in front of his cell and leaning on the railing, he found himself talking to a guy recently arrested on a petty charge and sent to the "junkie" floor. Dante soon realized this was the same wayward man whom his cellmate had mentioned and whom he had been praying for. "Often a wise God has to do a speedy and strange work in people that is not understood by others; like the prophets in the Old Testament who would obey God rather than men, they spoke and performed some very strange acts. This wino that God introduced me to helped me witness first-hand the amazing power of prayer."

As he continued speaking to the wino, Dante realized it was God who had brought them together. Dante knew that most people would think this was stupid. He knew he lived in a secular world that scoffed at God and especially at miracles. He knew that many people thought they were far too smart for God. He had been like that, telling others that self-reliance was the way, not reliance on somebody you couldn't even see. Others thought the Bible a fairy tale, the resurrection a clever ruse. For many, God was far away, if He was there at all, and He sure didn't enter your life in a personal way and start directing it. "It was unbelievable. At the time, I did not realize that God was performing an accelerated work with me," he said. "I was thirty-one years old and had spent almost two-thirds of it invested in things of the world. I usually was busted and sent to prison during the month of May. I remember trying to attach some spiritual significance to this, but to no avail."

Growing in Christ was not as easy as he first hoped. Although he was finally saved, it would take awhile before he could truly accept it. For the next few weeks, he found himself writing letters, mostly to himself, trying to describe what had happened. On one of the days that he had to go to court on the armed robbery charge, he wrote that, despite his fear of being given a long sentence, he continued to hear the cries of the lost. He couldn't ignore the pain and suffering of those around him and wanted to reach out to them. "Now I pray for extra strength to pull my brothers with me to the house of the Lord. Give us the strength, dear God, before the lost fall into the snares set for them by the wicked."

His conversion brought him peace, a feeling of having left the Inferno and even being on the periphery of Paradise, a state that puzzled his fellow inmates who had known him before. He no longer paced the tiers like an angry lion. He simply sat in his cell, staring serenely at the passing scene. They didn't know it, nor did he, that the conversion was real, just as real as the conversion that struck St. Paul off his horse on the way to Damascus. It was the pivotal point of Dante's life. "My friends worry over me because I seem to mourn," he wrote. But he was not feeling grief. Instead, "I seem to be filled with the Holy Spirit."

Yet, he was still bedeviled by doubt and some of the old, familiar emotions. "It is getting very uncomfortable here in my imprisonment," he wrote. "Lately, I've begun to think about my freedom." Try as he might, it was hard holding onto that sweet sense of floating that he experienced on the morning after his conversion.

Everywhere he went in the jail, he felt surrounded by a steamy restlessness that made him think of riots, of police clubs falling on heads. He was starting to see all of these as manifestations of an absence of God. At the same time, though, this was the summer of 1964, a time of widespread civil unrest across the country, including Harlem where a police officer had killed a teenager for no good reason. Hearing of the rioting out in the streets that followed the killing of the teenager, Dante took up his pen to write this poem.

JULY 19, 1964

Harlem is seething, Harlem is taut;
    What does Martin Luther King say?
He is our leader. What does he speak?
    Youth has been smacked
And the sting echoes through Harlem—
    What does Martin Luther King say?

Yesterday we won; today we lose a son.
    Hypocrisy, madness, or individualism?
Let us hear Martin Luther King—
    What does he say?

Oh God! Lead us not into temptation.
    We hurt!
Shotguns and bullets
    Have punctured and ripped
The white paper edict of our
    Earned civil rights.

Take our tears, take our cries.
    Mold them, Lord; they are your weapons.
Harlem is seething, Harlem is taut;
    What does Martin Luther King say?

As the outside world smoldered, there were times when he, too, was hot and angry. "I awaken speechless and nasty," he wrote. "And on these days I search my soul more deeply to find the truth. I look for a release from this compulsory madness." He found times when he couldn't even deal with intrusions from other inmates. "I snap because something born of the Holy Spirit and truth is not to be interrupted by mortal beings. When God speaks, no one interrupts." All in all, he was on a spiritual rollercoaster, trying to adjust to a new perspective. Doubt continued to dog him. He was all alone. There was no one to teach him on a daily basis about his new life and how to walk in the Lord. He had no idea that unexplained mood-swings were a normal part of the process for many new Christians. "It swings from one side to the other and it almost sends me back to confusion, but I hold fast until I swing back. Then I recognize the pattern and thank God I'm not lost."

15
CHANGE

One day three of Dante's friends—Pacheco, Gifucci and Malambo—were playing dominoes in the day room. Feeling in a pensive mood, Dante sat nearby, looking through the bars on the windows, when he heard Malambo say that they needed to find enjoyment in their lives, even when behind bars. Pacheco slammed a domino on the aluminum table, loudly agreeing with Malambo. "Having some fun," said Pacheco, "was as necessary to a man as was thinking." Gifucci then jumped in: "I think a man needs both, and also maintain his equilibrium, to function as a man."

Dante thought there was more to being a man than having fun, thinking, or staying on an even keel, and that something was God, but he didn't say anything. He kept looking out the window, gazing at the elevated Major Deegan Highway, and further on at the Harlem River Drive. From there, his mind wandered. Wasn't "Sugar Hill" out that way and beyond it, the projects, and City College? "And beyond that?" he asked himself, answering, "Who knows; perhaps the world began its curve there."

During this period, he seesawed back and forth on how to deal with the armed robbery charge. He wondered if he should keep quiet and let God handle it all. It might mean 40 years. Lying, he began to see, meant he was starting to turn his back against God. He decided, "I'm not going to lie for something I didn't do."

In plea bargaining, the authorities said, "Well, we'll give you a year."

Dante replied, "OK. I don't know about that."

"But when my mother walked into the courtroom, I saw that I was making her suffer. Why did I have to make her suffer some more?"

Then the judge asked, "Dante Venegas, how do you plead?"

"Because I was lying now, I said, 'God forgive me. Guilty.'"

The prosecuting attorney jumped up. "Your Honor, we cannot accept that plea! Either he's guilty or he's not guilty! God has nothing to do with this!" (*The Testimony*)

However, God had everything to with it. Dante's heart-felt prayers were realized. With the unconditional support of Rev. Daughtry and his mother, the sentence for the bogus armed robbery charge was plea-bargained down from 40 years to a year and a day. Dante reluctantly agreed to it. "Yes, in my darkness, I became aware of a light, and the light mortified all evil and attracted Truth and Love," he wrote.

On July 30, 1964 Dante was transferred to Rikers Island to serve his sentence of a year and a day. Upon arrival, he learned that Johnny B., his friend who had snitched on him in 1957 and gotten him those three years in Lewisburg Penitentiary, was there. Dante could hardly wait for his cell door to open so he could go find Johnny and tell him that he forgave him for that betrayal. After that, he did his time quietly, often reading the Bible and hoping to hold on to that feeling of being filled with the Holy Spirit. He also worked on and received his high school equivalency diploma, an accomplishment making him and his mother proud.

His mother, Sara, stood by him that entire time, even though his sister, Toni, was urging her to cut him loose. As a matter of fact, Dante's extended family was tired of him. His former sister-in-law recalled how they dreaded seeing him come around. He showed up unannounced, high on drugs, looking unkempt and pitiful, many of his teeth gone. He made them nervous because he was always snooping around for something to steal. Sara Venegas, however, never gave up on him. She had even spent money set aside for her retirement to keep Dante in touch with a good lawyer to fight the armed robbery charge. Dante knew his continuing incarcerations were taking their toll on her. When she came to see him, her eyes were dark from lack of sleep and her face sagged with sadness. Dante tried to assure her, though, that he had changed.

He reminded her how he had been in Rikers three years before. At that time, he said, he "was anxious to learn the art of deception and nimble fingers to carry myself through life." But now he was studying algebra, geography and English, working hard to catch up. And he might even go to college. "There is a different and deeper kind of knowledge that I crave," he told Sara. He wanted to know more about God and God's Word. That was real and lasting knowledge that would help him build a new life.

It's possible his mother did see an inkling of change. She loved him and always had, and didn't want to give up on him. Dante wrote poems about this, celebrating and honoring his mom. One day, she suggested that he attend a church when he got out. She may have suggested that Spanish Lutheran church where Dante had been confirmed.

1 Year—Rikers Island

No wonder I ache here of late.
    They have taken out beauty and instilled
Personality. Surely it's wrong.

Chattering autumn leaves merrily
    Play and chase each other around a
Lonely park bench, while my spirit
    Leans heavily against these prison
Walls, and aches.

They've even blocked my view,
    And now it's fortune to stand tip-toed
And glimpse my star or catch the rapid
    Journeys of our moon.

Anticipating sleep at the end of a
    Long and woeful day, I painfully hang
Up my mask. And every morning a whistle
    Brings me back. After blues and reds,
And vivid shades, a whistle brings me back
    To grey; from heavenly dreams to drab
And prison grey.

Once I soared to the rim of divinity
    And peeped. The truth, the beauty I
Beheld there was the power that projects
    Some to eternal and divine ground;
And I merely peeped. Now a whistle blows
    And brings me back to grey;
To drab and prison grey.

                    (Written by Dante in 1964
                    during his incarceration)

16

"BUY A TICKET"

When released from Rikers Island in 1965, Dante felt fragile and uncertain. While behind bars, there was no way to learn new strategies to help him when released. "No one taught me how to live a new and different lifestyle when I went back out on the streets," he said. Attempting to keep that connection to God, he could have gone to Rev. Daughtry's church, but didn't. Instead, he went almost straight to that Spanish Lutheran church. He slipped in, filled with the Holy Spirit and looking to connect with a community that worshipped God. He was happy and sat down, ready to hear the preacher speak the truth.

But then he looked around at the church. It was old and showing it. The smell of stale cigarettes hung in the air and he smelled stale whiskey on the breath of some people. No one welcomed him. He waited, trying to discern the Holy Spirit in the place, but he only began to feel rejected, empty and hopeless. If this was church, if this was how to worship God, he wanted none of it. Soon, he left. Darkness seemed to envelop him. The high hopes he had felt in jail seemed to evaporate. He began to doubt his salvation, wondering if it had simply been a jailhouse phenomenon. Devastated by his experience, his faith shaken to the core, self-destruction once again set in. Having learned no new coping skills, he resorted to the only thing he knew how to do—drugs. His father's words, telling him he was mediocre, resounded in his head. Maybe there was no way out for him.

This time he went back to the drugs with a vengeance. For one whole year, he committed more brazen crimes than at any other time in his life.

"But I could not get arrested. Now I was sticking up for real and didn't care. I didn't care who I sold dope to. 'Kill me!' I would walk into grocery stores with two shopping bags and go straight to the meat department. I'd look in the freezer, open up the bags and take roasts, and then walk out in broad daylight and start selling them to the people right outside. Now that's crazy! I wanted somebody to put a bullet in my head!" (*The Testimony*)

He was desperate, living without relief. He was on a roller-coaster, one day full of despair and the next wondering if he should try church again. Maybe there he could find the strength to kick this lifestyle.

One Sunday morning in 1966, he got dressed, determined to go to church and try to end the horror into which he had again plunged himself. Dabbing on cologne, he felt optimistic, leaving his apartment and heading for the subway. This time he would go to Rev. Daughtry's church. But a car came alongside him. Someone rolled down a window and called out to him. The car was filled with his doping buddies. It didn't take too much cajoling before he was in that car shooting up. The high started, but it wasn't enough. He needed more. He didn't stop, taking more dope until he passed out. He had overdosed and looked like he was dead. Scared and unsure of what to do, his friends dragged him out of the car and dumped his body in an abandoned building. They left him in a crumpled heap, certain that the dope had killed him.

When he awoke in the unfamiliar place, Dante took time to gather his wits. He replayed all that happened, thinking maybe he took too much dope so he might die. But he wasn't dead. Nearby the sounds of the city getting ready for the start of a new week reminded him that life was going on, with or without him.

Then he heard a voice, the same one that had come to him before, the one that broke through the bricks and iron of the prison walls to reach him. He recognized it as the Holy Spirit, who spoke to him and told him to go to Lexington, Kentucky, for the four months and 15 days rehabilitation program. There he would get the help he needed. This time he would have to buy a ticket to Kentucky on his own; this time the government wasn't sending him.

Dante wondered if he wanted the help, or if it would do any good. He kept getting straight, only to continue falling into one sewer or another. Still, he listened to the Holy Spirit insist on a plan of action. It became clear. God wanted him to enter rehab in Kentucky. For some reason, he didn't argue. "Buy a ticket and don't let anyone know you are going," he heard the Lord say as he slowly staggered home.

17

"GO HOME"

Scraping up what money he had, he bought a train ticket to the US Public Health Service prison/hospital at Lexington, where he'd been twice before, to get clean. When he arrived, he requested and was granted his wish to work outside in the sewage treatment plant. He was assigned to the filtration section of the Water Department. As it turned out, said Jackie, this job taught him a lesson and got him thinking. "As he watched, day to day, he began seeing the filtering process as a picture of God's grace in a person's life. The water entered dirty, sometimes black, filled with human waste and garbage. But as it proceeded through the varying stages of filtration, it became clearer and clearer until the finished product appeared pristine, pure and beautiful." Dante saw this filtration process as reflecting the restorative and redemptive work of God. The Lord, if Dante let it happen, would clean him up, too, sending him through the different processes that would bring him "to the beauty and purity of eternity."

One day, three months and 15 days into the program, Dante was working outside when he looked over to see that some cows had meandered from the pasture up to a fence near where he was doing his assigned job. The cows looked at him with big expectant eyes. Dante thought of what he wanted to do and got an idea. He took his well-worn New Testament out of his back pocket, waltzed up closer and began preaching to the cows, talking to them about the Lord, about how God purified even the dirtiest of his creatures. He never said how the cows responded or what text he used. But he did hear a voice, this one God's.

"Go home."

"But I've got to do four months and 15 days," Dante argued.

"I'm telling you to go home."

"But, but . . ."

"You're cured," God said.

"'Ohhh! Wow!' So I went and checked out, went to the train station, and the Devil was there." (*The Testimony*)

A woman sidled up to him and said, "Hi, baby. You want some cough syrup?"

"No thanks," he told her.

"Are you sure?" she asked coyly.

"Yes, I'm OK," Dante replied.

A while later, as he waited for the train, the woman returned with a bottle of Wild Irish Rose and asked if he wanted some. Again, he declined, aware that this woman was hitting on him and wanted more from him than just getting high.

Once he was on the train and feeling safe, she showed up again, sashaying down the aisle. She sat next to him, leaned close and told him she had some good heroin at home, and lots of it: 45 bags from Black Ross, a drug connection Dante knew and trusted.

"You can come and we can party. But you have to come in through the fire escape because I don't have my key."

Becoming somewhat annoyed, Dante replied, "No, I'm not interested in that."

He had been through this before, the misadventures and flimsy relationships between junkies. As he told her "No," he spotted another man, sitting a few seats up. The man was sneezing, but he also had a certain look about him—a mixture of hunger, dissolution, and desperation. Dante knew the guy was in need of a fix.

"See that brother over there? He needs some dope. Talk to him." To Dante's surprise and pleasure, she got up and went to sit next to the guy.

18
CHURCH

Soon after arriving in New York City, Dante headed straight for the House of the Lord Pentecostal Church, where Rev. Daughtry preached. This time he did not make the mistake of attending a church whose atmosphere was stale and whose memories, for Dante, were not good. Almost as soon as he arrived, he felt a power that he had missed in the other church. He knew that the Holy Spirit danced here and that religion was vital and alive.

From the pulpit, Rev. Daughtry roared out a message of salvation. He spun right and left, his arms waving, his black robes flapping. This was the soft-spoken man whom Dante had met in Lewisburg Penitentiary. This was the same man who had kept up a relationship and wrote to Dante, even sent him money, while he was behind bars. Daughtry had assured him, time and again, "God can change people. God can even change murderers into missionaries."

Dante was struck by the preaching and the atmosphere of his friend's church. He was especially moved by how the "old African American Mothers of the Church" began to surround him with love and acceptance. Instead of rejecting him, they wrapped their arms around him and began calling him "Brother Dante." They admonished him when he seemed to be straying and praised him highly when he showed how much the Lord was starting to mean to him. He loved the emotionalism, the exuberant prayer, and the music that grabbed him at the core of his soul. Pentecostal prayer made sense to him, since it came from deep inside of a person and was aimed directly at God. He stayed there for seven years, becoming an assistant of sorts to Rev. Daughtry who continued teaching him the Bible and giving him insight on being a pastor.

Dante was blessed with many experiences at the church, learning important principles about God and how He works. When the church was looking for a new facility, Dante went with Rev. Daughtry and two others to the site of a church building in Brooklyn on Atlantic Avenue. This was where they hoped to be able to move. They went there, though, not to negotiate with anyone in a worldly way over price. Instead, the four of them knelt on a sidewalk in front of the prospective church and prayed to God that He deliver the place to them. They had unabashedly claimed it in the name of Jesus and eventually the Lord answered their prayer by giving them the building as a new place of worship for the congregation.

19
SMALL BEGINNINGS

Dante loved to work. His first job, at the age of 13, was working as a Page in the NYC Public Library's Schomburg Center in Harlem, a job he loved because he got to handle and check through so many books. From that time on, even in times of trauma, he became a voracious and wide-ranging reader. And there were other jobs. While incarcerated at Hart Island, he planted trees in Potter's Field. He drove different types of delivery trucks, often being asked to cheat. He worked in a vinyl factory in New Jersey and clerked at the Post Office.

When he began attending Rev. Daughtry's church, he had taken a temporary job as a doorman at the upscale Lord & Taylor Department Store, where he had to wear a uniform. Looking so good and official in it, he turned out to be a big hit with the older ladies for whom he opened doors. One woman took the trouble to tell the boss what a great guy they had handling the doors leading in and out of the ritzy store. When Dante's time was up, they paid him and gave him a bottle of Scotch for doing so well. He recalls walking away that day, whistling, and with several hundred dollars of tips in his pocket. Life was good. He gave the bottle of Scotch away, but he was happy to be able to drop his first tithe in the offering basket at House of the Lord Church.

Also in this period, he was back to dating Black Rose, and Rev. Daughtry asked him to bring her with him to church one Sunday, which he did. "I believe if more so-called Christians had the level of commitment and respect that Daughtry had for lost souls, the kingdom of God would expand exponentially," says Dante. Black Rose apparently enjoyed the service, but she didn't join up as did Dante. Her religion was darker, full of good and bad spirits. It was more animistic, without any real solid connection to Jesus. Eventually, she drifted from Dante as his religion seemed to take over and fill his life.

Dante says his sudden and almost inexplicable conversion left him with many questions, some of which Rev. Daughtry was able to answer, or at least point him in the right direction. He learned the importance of memorizing the Word of God, for instance, by sitting down at the dinner table with Rev. Daughtry's family. Dante says he was pre-warned that everyone who ate dinner at his table must recite a verse of Scripture before eating. Dante was nervous, especially when he was handed a King James Bible and told, "You still have time to find and memorize a verse."

Dante searched for the shortest one he could find. It didn't take long. He found a verse, Matthew 8:20, memorized it and recited: "Foxes have holes, and birds of the air have nests; but the Son of man has nowhere to lay His head." Dante had no great revelation or understanding at the time of what the passage meant. But it got him dinner.

Pentecostal worship always resonated with him, and he attended the highly expressive services at different churches on and off throughout his life. At the same time, though, he eventually began to feel a need to be taught a more systematic approach to God. Basically, he needed a teacher to disciple him and guide him in how to best express his faith in words. Little did he know then exactly where that discipleship would eventually come from and where it would lead.

20
PASTRAMI

During his years as an addict, Dante would drop in every so often at the Addicts Rehabilitation Center (ARC), operating at that time out of a small office in the Manhattan Christian Reformed Church, which was housed in a large, old 5-story building at the corner of Seventh Avenue and 122nd Street in Harlem. Dante was drawn there to pass the time, rest in the pews, play chess and talk with fellow addicts. "He was a big, good-looking guy," says Rev. Gordon Negen, who took over after Rev. Eugene Callender, the first African-American to be ordained in the CRC, left. "Dante was very talented and articulate. It was obvious to me that he was a cut above, but he didn't really come to services."

Initially, ARC was a loose-knit group, coming and going as they chose, supervised by James Allen, an ex-addict and member of the church. He came there in 1958 and found solid support in the then-pastor, Rev. Callender. In 1960, Allen was hired full-time by the church to work with addicts. He eventually moved out of the church building in the mid 1960s and set up a drug rehabilitation facility on 123rd Street. Some years later, ARC moved to Park Avenue and 128th Street.

Dante landed a full-time job early in 1967 as a receptionist with Allen's ARC after the rehab center had moved from the church. He liked Mr. Allen's easygoing but no-fooling-around personality and was pleased when Allen offered him the position. With his quick wit and winning personality, Dante was popular at the front desk. He welcomed everyone and was especially sensitive to the needs of addicts who might stumble in, still full of dope, their eyes hazy, halfheartedly looking for help. "Dante was always lifting people's spirits," says Allen, who is still active in ARC. "When things were rough, Dante always had a wisecrack to get us out of it. At the same time, he was one of the smartest, keenest guys I ever knew." Because of his talent for reaching out to addicts in a way they could accept, Dante left the reception desk and became a counselor. Allen says people around ARC still remember Dante and the piece titled "What's a Pastrami?" that he wrote in the Center's July 1968 newsletter.

"Pastrami" became an inside joke after the article appeared. Essentially, it revolved around the authority that Mr. Allen had. What he said was the gospel, and that was an important lesson for self-absorbed addicts to learn. In his article, Dante recounts how Allen confronted a candidate for the program, asking him, "What is a pastrami?" Not sure how to react, the candidate shot a furtive glance around the room, looking to others for help. None was offered. Face expressionless, Mr. Allen asked again, "What is a pastrami, man?" Realizing that he wasn't going to get any help in answering this simple but puzzling question, the guy said it was a sandwich. Allen smiled and slowly shook his head, "No." The guy was by now thoroughly confused, looking like he was ready to chalk up his plea for residency and continue taking his chances in the nether world of addiction. His shoulders slumped and he said, "Man, if pastrami is not a sandwich, then I don't know what it is." The guy threw up his hands and looked out a window, ready to leave this crazy place.

Then Mr. Allen said kindly, "Come here, my man, and I'll tell you what a pastrami is. It is a sexy little three-legged animal." This really hit the guy in the wrong place. "A what?" he just about screamed. "A sexy little three-legged animal," Allen said softly. The guy thought about it a moment. It made no sense to him. And then, writes Dante, he asked the question that would start his process toward sobriety. "Oh yeah, why?"

This was the key! Asking "why" got the therapeutic process in gear. Addicts are so self-absorbed that they rarely listen to anyone else about anything. Allen simply responded, "Because I said so," and left the room.

The guy didn't get it right away—that he was there and had to follow directions. Mr. Allen was the boss, and the counselors were not far behind. There was an important lesson here: If you want to get better, stop listening to yourself. You are not in charge. Your addiction got the better of you. You need to surrender and start listening to others.

"Always after that," writes Dante, "rationalization, petty excuses, sudden mysterious ailments all disappear when a mandate is issued from the executive director's office." When addicts would question "Why this?" or "Why that?" the answer they were given, and still receive today, was "Pastrami." In other words, it was because Mr. Allen said so. Dante had reduced a complex therapeutic intervention down to one word. The word "Pastrami" spoke the philosophy of the program.

21
JACKIE

Dante sat on a bench along the Hudson River. He and Jackie Mulder, a youth worker at Manhattan Christian Reformed Church, were poring over parts of the Bible. She was helping him see how the Bible was a set of stories that had, starting with the Old Testament and moving into the New Testament, an overarching quality of salvation, fraught with human longing and suffering. They made sense, moving from the Garden of Eden to the cross on Calvary and beyond. As boats passed on the river and the huge city seemed to rise all around them, they spoke. Dante asked questions, and Jackie answered them as well as she could. He was dark-skinned and streetwise, and she was white and not really familiar with the ways of places like Harlem, Brooklyn and the Bronx. At first, he had no interest in her at all. "And the next thing I knew, we sat down and began to read the Word of God," he said.

Reading the Bible was only one of the activities they shared as they sat by the river. They watched the river traffic, particularly the tugboats, which fascinated Dante. "The tugboat seemed to provide him with a philosophical and spiritual point," says Jackie. "The smallest, most unattractive, seemingly unimportant—this was the boat with immense power, working in the background as an essential part of keeping the Hudson and East Rivers free and effective at moving cargo and ships along the flowing waters."

They had met at ARC in early 1967. Dante was working as a receptionist and, on her way to assist James Allen with a project, she was struck by Dante's welcoming smile and they talked briefly. Jackie, a college graduate, had come to New York City as part of the CRC Home Missions teacher volunteer program that sent people to mission sites all over the country. While Jackie was struck by Dante's charismatic personality, he wasn't sure what to make of her—this small, slender, pretty blonde from the Midwest. At first, he didn't see her as a possible marriage partner. Dante had always envisioned that he would marry a Puerto Rican woman with long dark hair and luscious features. But there he was on the bench, studying the Bible with this woman with whom he felt he had little in common.

They had a bond centered on religion and Christ that drew them together. Jackie was impressed with his "on-fire faith even though he was a young Christian." Dante was curious and especially eager to know more about the Christian Reformed Church (CRC).

Dante recalled one day sitting in Manhattan CRC, while Jackie was at a rehearsal, when he grabbed a *Psalter Hymnal* from behind one of the pews and began to idly page through it. He checked out some of the songs, but then reached the back of the book that contained the Doctrinal Standards of the Christian Reformed Church. The first section grabbing his attention was The Heidelberg Catechism, one of the standards of faith and unity in the CRC. Among other things, he read Q&A 1: "What is your only comfort in life and death?" The answer: "That I am not my own, but belong—body and soul, in life and in death—to my faithful Savior Jesus Christ. He has fully paid for all my sins with his precious blood, and has set me free from the tyranny of the devil." Man, that answer hit him in the solar plexus. What profound wisdom and comfort it offered! The catechism fired his mind: it put into words so much of what he felt, providing a framework on which to continue to build his faith. "I found the creeds of the CRC to be so refreshing and to reflect what I was thinking. The Heidelberg Catechism turned me on to the Reformed faith." Finally putting down the hymnal, Dante asked Jackie: "Do these people really believe this? This is gold!"

Surprised to hear what he said, Jackie replied: "Yes, they do." It was part of the Reformed faith, an approach to religion that was systematic and thorough. It had sound reasoning and Scriptural support for what the faith professed. Dante couldn't believe it. This was a church with a rock solid theology. It helped explain things that had confused him for years. In a letter many years later to his sister, Dante said this was "the way to go. As long as you digest it for yourself, you will be OK. Make sure you memorize the first Question and Answer: 'What is my only comfort in life and in death?'"

22

LINKED BY GOD

Dante loved Rev. Herbert Daughtry's church; it fed his spirit; the expressive worship was crucial to him. He resonated with the outpourings he heard and experienced. He loved the Pentecostal belief in the laying on of hands, in healing, in intercessory prayer and living the Spirit-filled life. While deeply touching his heart and soul, after a period of time, he wanted more to feed his active mind and to serve his personal learning style that needed a structured approach. The Reformed tradition seemed to offer some of that. All along, he had been studying the Bible. He bought a copy of the Good Book and kept going over and over it, making notations on the pages. He did the same with different editions of the Bible over the years, reading and scratching comments and reflections in the margins and underlining passages that spoke to him. It was a living document that never ceased to enlighten, challenge and comfort him. While he relied on Daughtry for many answers, he questioned and received support from many others as well, especially at ARC.

Deep as he was into studying the Bible, Dante wasn't sure he wanted to get involved with Jackie, this woman from Grand Rapids, Michigan. They were from such different cultures. Each wondered if they could bridge the enormous cultural gap between them and transcend their different backgrounds. Dante was a black Puerto Rican from Spanish Harlem. Jackie was a white member of the CRC denomination, a church of more than 200,000 members in the United States and Canada that was known, at least in the 1960s, to be Dutch to the core of its DNA. While they both had doubts, many of their friends—especially Richard Feimster, Deputy Director of ARC, and his wife Elease—said they were meant to be together. Theirs was a relationship ordained by God. Others agreed with them.

Dante asked her out on their first date in the summer of 1967, and then he didn't show. Yet, he kept being drawn to Jackie as a kind of odd soul mate. They had their first official date over lunch at a place near ARC. He had no idea how to talk to a "square" girl, so their conversation turned to talking about the Lord. And in that way, the relationship grew.

Given that this was the 1960s, and the U.S. Supreme Court had finally ended all race-based legal restrictions on marriage in 1967, there was concern among CRC officials whether Jackie was making the right move. A group of representatives from Christian Reformed Home Missions made the unusual move of coming out to talk to her in 1968, wanting to get a sense of how serious the two were. Although the team from the church was not happy with the match, fearing negative repercussions throughout the denomination, it did nothing to stop it. Ironically, Dante and Jackie had broken up at this point, and Jackie had made plans to return to Michigan to attend graduate school. She was teaching at JHS 123 in the Bronx at the time.

Before they had called things off, Dante couldn't get her out of his mind. Among other things, besides her beauty, he saw in Jackie a purity of purpose that he lacked. He kept talking to her, becoming more and more comfortable with her and her interest in the city he grew up in. He showed her some of his old haunts, had her meet his friends—one of whom was Alphonse Brown, known as Ahmad, a wise and nutty jazz lover, a songwriter and a true Bohemian. They visited him for a couple of hours one day in Ahmad's flat on Mt. Morris Park W. near 121st Street. After awhile, Ahmad told Dante, "Jackie is the one for you." In years previous, Dante had brought other girl friends by to meet him. But Ahmad always said about the others, "No, this isn't the one for you."

Ahmad was not religious, but he did seem to have a mystical connection to the world of the spirit that enabled him to "see" things. Because of the respect he held for Ahmad, Dante often went to him to talk over important decisions. In many ways, their mutual love for jazz and poetry united them. At one point, Ahmad even predicted that Dante would one day "wear soft shoes and carry a Bible," and this was long before Dante's salvation. Seer that he could be, Ahmad saw something else in Dante: his ease with people and his winning personality. He was always amazed, says Jackie, how easily people took to Dante. "Dammit, Dante, everybody likes you!" he exclaimed.

The breakup between Dante and Jackie lasted for several months. Despite the obstacles, they pressed on, even when Jackie left to finish her Master's degree at the University of Michigan. During this period, Dante sent her many poignant letters, unburdening his heart, becoming aware as he wrote, and starting to tell her, how much he loved and needed her and how she provided balance in his life. Their relationship solidified from afar, held together more and more by their individual devotion to Jesus Christ. They began to see their way through to a life together. In his letters to Ann Arbor, Dante hinted at marriage, trying to gauge her thoughts.

When Jackie returned in 1969 and began working as a counselor for the NYC Public Schools, they continued to date and got married a year later. For a class he was taking, Dante wrote that he was not too keen on marriage as an institution. He believed society itself promoted divorce, not stable marriages. "We seem to live in a society which fosters alienation: a me, me, and me syndrome is apparent to many of us. In a society full of techniques and gimmicks, no one ever wants to take the time to really know one another." He and Jackie broke this trend by slowly getting to know and move closer to one another. And always it was God that centered them. They were well aware how the godlessness of the world played into marital problems. "I believe the divorce rate in our country reflects more than just the abandonment of marriage vows and purposes. Its root cause goes back to the abandonment of God's laws—alienation from God first, then alienation from His purposes, marriage included," Dante wrote.

Despite his early misgivings, Dante came to believe that he and Jackie were linked by God, and that they had a chance to make it as a bi-racial couple. He knew it would be hard work and challenging, but he had begun to cherish Jackie and wanted to be with her for the rest of his life. She was no Black Rose, often bombastic, frequently on the move toward better things in the world. She was no luscious Puerto Rican. She was a lovely blond woman from West Michigan, perky, funny, serious, and one to speak her mind. Plus, she played a mean piano. Amazed as he was to be marrying this woman from Grand Rapids, he realized that she had won his heart. They had broken up, only to become a couple again. In a pre-marriage poem, he says, "Oh glad I am that I have not wed. I've seen the joy and sorrow." In other words, he was ready to make the commitment. Years on the streets and in prison played a role in his preparation.

They were married on July 11, 1970 in a small ceremony conducted by Jackie's father, Rev. John Mulder, a long-time CRC preacher. But this was not before Dante gained his future father-in-law's approval for the marriage. Dante passed muster when he was able to recite word for word the Apostle's Creed, learned so many years before in that Spanish Lutheran church.

23
DANTE'S EXAMPLE

A couple of years into their marriage, Dante began attending services more frequently at Manhattan Christian Reformed Church. He ended up leading a men's group, which included a weekly Saturday breakfast and Bible study. His knowledge and passion for the Word, coupled with what he was beginning to see as a sense of calling to some sort of ministry, led him from the men's group into the full life of the church. Rev. James White, pastor at Manhattan CRC for several years starting in 1969, recalls that the men's group included well-dressed African American men who were protégés of the well-known Harlem gangster, Bumpy Johnson, as well as street-corner-men. People from all walks and stations of life were drawn to Dante and how he taught the Bible. "Dante came across as authentic. Whatever he said, the men embraced it," said White, who grew up in Harlem and taught for a time at Calvin College before getting into politics in the city of Grand Rapids. "The men in that group responded to Dante in a way that told me he should be a minister. Watching him enabled me to see what God had gifted him with."

When White left in the mid-1970s to teach at Trinity Christian College in Illinois, the church was left without a full-time pastor. Various CRC preachers were assigned pulpit duty. Without a steady pastoral presence, the church began to flounder. Seeing that the church was lacking direction and a firm spirit, Dante found himself becoming more involved. Having joined the church a few years after marrying Jackie, he became an elder and began teaching and then preaching. From the pulpit, he brought a Pentecostal fire that drew people back to the church. But that doesn't mean he ignored the Reformed imperatives. One CRC pastor recalls being asked to preach at the church. Before he was allowed to take the pulpit, Dante grilled him at length about the topic and gist of the sermon, making sure that it fit within the orthodoxy, as he then understood it, of the CRC while also being appropriate for the church.

After Dante's death, the church, now known as the Christian Parish for Spiritual Renewal, sent condolences to his family. "We want you to know that, although his body has left this place, his spirit, his love and his impact are still alive, well and flowing through the veins of this ministry. Well done, thou good and faithful servant."

While remaining active in the church, Dante continued working with addicts, helping them to change their lives through the power of God. For him, this work was as much a ministry as it was a way to make a living. After leaving ARC, Dante was on staff from 1969–1978 at Brookdale Hospital in Brooklyn, where he worked in the Department of Psychiatry as a counselor and drug-treatment specialist. Brookdale, a teaching hospital, was very influential in Dante's development and growth in his newfound life. They trusted him, treating him as an equal, seeing in him the genius he had for working with others, and giving him responsible positions from the beginning. They were not put off by the fact that he had no degree. "I was supervising people with Master's degrees, and I only had a GED," he said in wonderment.

He also took courses there in psychology and was trained by Dr. G. Puglisi, a psychiatrist from Italy, to run therapeutic groups. Dante became an excellent and highly respected group therapist. "Brookdale recognized his giftedness and invested a lot in him," says Jackie. "The information and skills he learned there provided the basis for his effectiveness in ministry."

He worked with the hardest mentally ill ex-convicts and addicts that the teaching hospital could provide. One group, for example, contained a very large, hardened, angry man who was blind and had just completed a 30-year sentence for murder. One day this man came to the group very angry.

"Dante, I'm going to set that bus driver straight! He refused to drive a couple of blocks out of the way to drop me off."

"You sure got some nerve, man," Dante laughingly replied. "You're blind, and if you threaten the driver, he could easily take you to some isolated place and drop you off in the boondocks. You would have no idea where you were. Think about that before you make your decision."

By the time the group ended, the man thanked Dante for his wisdom. Dante was the one on staff who did not fear these guys or confronting them; he had a way they responded to. His superiors were often surprised and pleased by how well he could step into the world of even the sickest mind and help that person make sense out of things. Dante was beginning to see that he could return to the dark places, as long as he had God along for protection.

Dante did not limit his concern for the guys to his workweek. Often on Saturdays, he took his family with him to go check on someone who was having a rough time, or to bring a homemade meal to a junkie experiencing "the chucks," or just to walk the mean streets sharing kindness and concern for society's rejects, thereby validating their humanity. "We found ourselves in some really scary and threatening places," says Jackie. "But as long as Dante showed confidence, the girls and I were not afraid. The more we did this, the more and more comfortable we became in many different types of settings. We have fond memories of those times and feel very blessed to have had those experiences."

Jack Wooster, who lives in Brooklyn, can attest to Dante's effective and caring approach. He met Dante when they lived in the same high-rise apartment building located just down the street from Brookdale. Jack was a hard case, deep into booze when he met Dante through his own wife who was friends with Jackie; also, their daughters were playmates. Seeing a man in need of help, Dante didn't push but took him along to a few places he had to visit for his job. Although Dante badly wanted to help Jack get sober, he knew that was up to God. Dante didn't want himself to be so loud that Jack couldn't hear God speaking to him. Dante took him to an old movie theater that served as a rehabilitation center in the Bedford Stuyvesant section of Brooklyn. There was a large sign "TRY" hanging on the outside. They toured it and at the end, Dante asked, "So, what'd you think?" Jack replied, "It's a nice place. Let's go." Jack wasn't ready, and Dante didn't press the matter, simply allowing Jack to make up his own mind.

"Dante never told me what to do. He was the one who gently showed me I was in serious trouble. He got me to see that I was responsible for my soul," says Jack. "Dante was not a mysterious person at all. He was a very robust man and said what he wanted to say. But he was very sly, the way he would talk to me about my alcoholism."

In 1978, not long before Dante left Brooklyn and took his family to Grand Rapids, Jack recalls one day telling him how badly he felt, how the addiction was getting the best of him. Gazing at him, Dante said simply, "If you can't do it anymore, then you should stop." These were simple, no-nonsense words, but they were what Jack needed to hear at the time. Words, though, weren't what got him in the end. "The power of Dante's example is the only thing that reached me. For me, I took my first big step toward recovery just by being around him." Jack is more than 30 years sober today, attends a 12-step program and works as a carpenter in New York City.

24
STRONG MESSAGES

Working at Brookdale and adjusting to this new thing called marriage helped settle Dante down, but not totally, especially in the early days. Because he had not yet learned how to manage money, he got in a bind. Knowing no other way to make a few quick bucks, he sold pot and returned home to the Bronx with the proceeds in a guitar case. "Jackie, come here. Look what I've got!" he said excitedly. He opened the case and Jackie was shocked to see it full of money. Things were so dire then that, at times, Jackie's only option was to pick up coins off the streets and use them to buy food. But she wouldn't touch the guitar case. "Please close it," she told him. "I refuse to use one penny of this ill-gotten money. We need to bring this back to where you got it. Right now!"

Dante was perplexed by her reaction, but at 10 p.m. they piled their two daughters—Andrea and Michele, born in the first two years of their marriage—into the car to return the money to the supplier of the drug. That necessitated a 52-mile round trip from the Bronx to Brooklyn and back. God was definitely in the mix that evening. There was no anger. Only resignation of who they were together and the changes that needed to be made if they were going to make it. Jackie says she is aware that she provided stability and direction for Dante, and yet he offered her something she craved. He provided her with wings. "Together we could soar while still being grounded; that's what made us a team," she says.

Making the transition to such a totally different lifestyle wasn't easy for Dante. "There was a problem in his early years of being a Christian," says Jackie. "Even though he was learning the Word, was filled with the Spirit, and had developed Christian friends, when the 'rubber hit the road' out in the streets of life, he had difficulty applying and using the Word as a weapon."

He fought the evil that beset him with his own inner strength, but eventually found that strength waning and slowly began to panic. This happened after the family had moved to Brooklyn and during a time that Dante had started hanging around with an old friend, Sonny C., a different Sonny than the one he wanted to pattern himself after as a teenager. "They had met in Lewisburg Penitentiary, had run into each other occasionally over the years, and re-established a friendship when Sonny was hired as a counselor in Brookdale's Methadone program," says Jackie. Sonny initially seemed interested in religion and asked questions.

But gradually their conversation drifted from religion and they started hanging out more and more after work, a source of growing concern to Jackie as she could see how Dante was being negatively influenced. The Inferno, those licking flames, always so close, was threatening him again. Torn by the different aspects of his personality that were pulling him in different directions, he might have recalled a verse in a book he knew intimately, the *Divine Comedy*:

> Now here, now there, now down, now up again
>   it (hurricane) tosses them, uncomforted by hope
>   of any rest, nor even of less pain.
>
>   *The Inferno*, "*Canto V*"

Dante felt the pain of spiritual uncertainty described by his namesake. At some point, he realized how far he had begun to drift from the moorings of his faith and of his family. Likely it was this connection to Sonny and how close he came to once again being consumed by life on the streets that brought Dante to a state of hopelessness and despair. He knew that he was moving in the wrong direction—to the place where he had been before, a terrible place "uncomforted by hope."

Feeling frantic and fearful, he knew he had to turn back from the flames starting once again to singe his soul. He climbed into his car and drove in a panic to seek help from Rev. Ernest Trueblood, one of his Christian friends and mentors. When Dante arrived at International Revival Tabernacle, a small Spanish Pentecostal church near his home, Rev. Trueblood was standing in front of the building. Convinced that he had lost his connection to God, Dante began weeping. Through deep sobs and heaving breaths, he spoke these anguished words: "Brother Trueblood, I feel like the Holy Spirit has left me!" Rev. Trueblood put his arm around him and said, "Brother Dante, if the Holy Spirit has left you, you would not be weeping!"

This was a major revelation to Dante, and the two went inside the church. There, lying prostrate on the altar, they prayed, wept and cried out to God for deliverance. Dante felt the presence of the Holy Spirit arising within him, offering assurance that God had not forsaken him. He wrestled once again through confession and repentance. By his honesty and heart-felt pleas for help, he was able to get "back on track with the Lord." So when the Spirit of God had led him to pray with his friend and mentor, who ministered God's grace and mercy to him, there was great rejoicing in the Venegas household that evening. "We thanked God for His incomparable love, power, and deliverance," says Jackie.

A couple of months later, the telephone rang and Dante heard these hysterical words: "Dante, Sonny's dead! They found his body lying in the street, holding his keys in his hand." The stunning, sobering reality shook him hard. That could have been him, lying dead on some street, his bloody head in a gutter. Dante often said, "I need strong messages." Afflicted with Attention Deficit Hyperactivity Disorder (ADHD), a condition that would be diagnosed many years later, Dante needed messages that could break through the cacophony of his ever-moving, thought-scattered mind. This was a strong message, a message not lost on him. Death waited right around the corner if he went back to his old ways. He then asked himself how he could protect himself so that what happened to Sonny didn't occur in his life. As so often happened, he read the answer in the Bible. The message: "Be self-controlled and alert. Your enemy the devil prowls around like a roaring lion looking for someone to devour. Resist him, standing firm in the faith." (I Peter 5:8–9, NIV)

This experience underscored what Dante confronted with Rev. Trueblood's help and he had come to believe: No-one is above falling into sin and moving away from God. A person needs always to be alert to the possibility of yielding to temptation. At the same time, when someone falls, who has the right to judge? Dante knew that judgment and criticism were not the approaches to take. He would teach, telling other preachers in years to come how to deal with someone who has fallen into sin. He did this by quoting Galatians 6:1 (NIV), "You who are spiritual should restore him gently. But watch yourself, or you also may be tempted." Acutely aware of his humanness, Dante finally realized, in the wake of Sonny's death, that he had choices to make and yet could always rely on God as he made them.

Slowly but surely, he began to own up to and accept what he had been sensing for a long time: a calling to full-time ministry. But he had never attended seminary. For that matter, he hadn't amassed enough credits to earn a college degree. He had, however, finally left his life as a drug addict/criminal behind. Hanging onto the Lord kept him straight. He had started to feel the stirrings of a new vocation inside of him. He loved the Lord and wanted to tell others about it.

25
ANSWERED PRAYERS

Dante's mother, Sara, would come from Puerto Rico to visit and then ended up living with them in Brooklyn for a time. During this period, Dante worked at Brookdale and underwent a transformation into married life, becoming a dependable husband and father and a solid Christian. Even though Sara had married Dante's excitable and profane father, she always maintained her deep faith and an active prayer life, which she passed on to her son.

"Dante's love for his mother was a beautiful thing to behold," says Jackie. Over time, she began to realize that "in the middle of the chaos in which he grew up, Sara was his rock." Dante cared deeply for her and always spoke lovingly of her. They created a bond back in his childhood that couldn't be broken, and only got more solid as the years went by. She prayed unceasingly for him, asking God to give her son a better future, always hopeful that God would hear her plea and make a difference in her son's life. God heard her prayers. His answer came unexpectedly one night in the form of a phone call to the Venegas home in 1978.

Dante picked up the phone. The call came from Rev. David Sieplinga, who had been a student pastor in 1970 on a temporary assignment from Calvin Theological Seminary to the Manhattan CRC, working under Rev. James White, when he and Dante got to know one another and became friends. While in Harlem, Sieplinga recognized that Dante had exceptional gifts for ministry and had been among those who stood behind him and encouraged him forward on a path that would turn him into a pastor. At the same time, Dante considered Dave a good friend, although he had considered him a naïve white man, totally unfamiliar with the challenges of Harlem, and yet wise in the ways of theology. As a trade-off, Dave taught him some Reformed doctrine and Dante took Dave around to different churches and introduced him to people, educating him about being an urban pastor. After Dave left to finish seminary and then moved on to take a church in Omaha, Nebraska, Dante spoke occasionally to him over the phone. Those conversations had been quite simple, basically catching up with one another. This time the call was serious.

Now calling from Grand Rapids, where he had been hired to pastor Madison Square Christian Reformed Church, a small Southeast Side church, Sieplinga didn't spend a great deal of time on small talk. "Dante, I want you to come to Grand Rapids and interview to work as my co-pastor," Sieplinga said.

Dante burst out laughing—his loud, hilarious, so-famous laugh, one that echoed throughout the apartment. Sieplinga had to be kidding. No way could he even consider this. And yet . . . maybe this call was an answer to prayer. That very day, Dante had been fasting and praying fervently, seeking direction for God's will in his life.

By this time, he had started to move away from the Pentecostal Church as Rev. Daughtry's ministry had taken a turn that was right for him, but not for Dante. Starting in the 1960s, Rev. Daughtry involved himself in many social justice issues in and around New York City. He was often on the front lines of pickets and sit-ins, protesting things such as police brutality. He was frequently quoted in the news over struggles he had with the local Orthodox Jewish community and politicians at City Hall. Dante went with him on some of these protests and joined him in some of his advocacy work. But he began sensing a calling in another direction. Although he agreed with the need for struggling publicly for civil rights, Dante didn't see his as a high-profile social justice ministry. While they maintained a friendship, it eventually became clear to him that Rev. Daughtry had received a special anointing and calling as a leader/pastor in the Civil Rights movement. Dante gradually grew to realize that he had been called to something very different. "There was no doubt that the Lord had called and gifted him to be an evangelist. His first concern was always for people's salvation and then growing in discipleship," says Jackie. "Dante had an incredible gift and passion for talking with people about the Lord—anyone, anywhere, at any time."

As a result, he wondered if the out-of-the-blue call from Sieplinga was the answer to which direction God wanted him to follow. Although having little idea of what he would face, Dante asked: "What's that mean for me, Dave?"

"Come here, meet with the Church Council, and give a sermon."

26
MADISON SQUARE CRC

Dante wasn't totally surprised or set back by the notion of moving to Grand Rapids. The city had been on his mind because Pastor James White several years earlier had been talking to him about studying for the ministry at Calvin Theological Seminary. A graduate of the seminary, White had even made inquiries to see if the seminary would be able to accommodate Dante and his special gifts.

After a little more conversation with Rev. Sieplinga, Dante said he would need to call him back. Then, following counsel from others and discussion and prayer with his wife and daughters, Dante called Dave back. He told him that he would be willing to check it out. Sieplinga's initial call came in July. Jackie says she did not want to move back to Grand Rapids, but believed she needed to keep her concerns to herself in order that her husband could clearly hear if God was calling him to Madison Square. She knew that if she told him how she felt, it would cause Dante hardship in making his decision.

Prior to Dante's interview, the congregation had experienced some challenges. Organized as a full-fledged CRC in 1970, Madison Square saw its ministry as reaching out to the population, mostly African American, who lived in nearby neighborhoods. Besides that, it began to develop a vision for being the church that welcomed people who didn't "fit" into the more traditional CRC.

In 1974 the church hired Rev. Virgil Patterson, one of the first African American pastors in the CRC. But, for various reasons, he resigned in 1977. Rev. Sieplinga was hired to replace him. Wanting to be multicultural, seeing the necessity of it in a quickly changing global world, the Church Council decided to act on Sieplinga's suggestion of meeting with his friend from New York City. In an emergency session, the Church Council decided to contact Dante.

He visited in August, and by September, they made him an offer to be co-pastor with Sieplinga. The offer threw him into a painful quandary. Jackie was adamant. She did not want to return to Grand Rapids. Yet, she too thought that the offer came from God and that becoming a CRC pastor might be the thing he was supposed to do. She told Dante, "If you hear the Lord calling you to go, then I know He will prepare my heart for the move."

In response to God's call on his life, Dante accepted the offer. As they prepared to leave, a major concern arose. Jackie said, "If you go out there talking about yourself as an ex-junkie and an ex-con, that's all you'll ever be. That title will always be associated with you and you won't be able to rise above it." Dante agreed totally. After prayer and much deliberation, they devised a strategy. He would not speak about his drug use or incarcerations to start, until people got to know him and see how he operated. Then he would start sharing his full story and, they believed, people would listen to it differently.

Knowing that Dante could talk himself out of accepting the call, or that Jackie might do it for him, Sieplinga didn't hesitate once he got a "yes." Because Madison Square at that time had few resources and no extra cash, Sieplinga went out and in a day raised enough money from five Grand Rapids-area businessmen to rent a moving truck and pay for gas. Accompanied by Vince Bivins, a member of the church, they drove straight out East to Brooklyn, giving Dante little time to reconsider. They were there within 24 hours to help the family put their belongings in the truck for the move. Once they arrived in Grand Rapids, the Venegas family stayed for a time in Sieplinga's house.

"One of my first impressions upon arriving in Grand Rapids from New York City in 1978 was that Martin Luther King Jr. had not been here," Dante recalls. "Until then, my whole life had been spent in New York City, an intense cauldron of ethnicities, rivalries and activities that blended in a way that worked sometimes and then sometimes flew right apart."

Grand Rapids was a town where racism existed, but not as overtly as it showed its ugly face elsewhere. "The great Martin Luther has affected all of Protestantism, but Martin Luther King Jr., the man who prophetically eulogized that he wanted to be remembered merely as the one 'who tried to love somebody,' had not yet impacted the 'Jerusalem' of the Christian Reformed Church," says Dante.

Madison Square Church, though, was ready to try to expand beyond its Dutch identity. Right in the heart of Grand Rapids, it became one of the first to attempt to break the mold, and did so slowly, and some say successfully. Dante was for many a wild card, a man of mystery, an unpredictable pastor, and some people labeled him a "duck out of water." But he didn't listen to the critics, even if what they said hurt and made him feel discouraged. Dante stayed. Eventually more and more people saw that indeed he might fit.

"It wasn't long before Pastor Dante touched everyone," says Louise Price, a teacher who began attending Madison soon after Dante arrived. "There was a special, anointed spirit in him. In many ways, Pastor Dante became a representation of Jesus' love to the people of Madison. He always encouraged, cared for and comforted people. He gave counsel and answered difficult questions. He gave us permission to not be perfect and yet still feel loved by our Lord. Pastor Dante's transparency in the pulpit added authenticity to his preaching. Using real-life experiences and situations to illustrate his sermon points made the Scriptures come alive. His frequent use of picture language has enabled many to remember sermon points even to this day. Most of all, his love for and exuberant joy in the Lord were contagious."

The early years at Madison Square CRC.

Andrea, Jackie, Dante and Michele

27
CHALLENGES

As he began his ministry at Madison Square CRC, Dante was effusive and genuinely interested in the people: Everyone from the long-time church organist to the farmer who drove into church from his celery and onion fields outside of the city. Perhaps because of Dante, and because of Sieplinga's clear support of his associate pastor, the church started to grow and add minority members, starting to form a face that reflected the many sides of God, in the midst of poverty, drug-related violence and alcohol and drug addiction.

"He was just like a brother to our family," says Molly Jefferson, a church member whose mother Dante adopted as his own and visited often, many times to eat breakfast and to talk over his troubles. Dante called her Mama Lu. "Pastor Dante was approachable. You could say anything to him. He helped make an about-face with that church," says Molly. "Out in the streets, he was considered a 'man among men,' a man whose presence lifted people above their circumstances, if even for only a moment. People loved being in his presence because they knew they would be touched in some way. He was 'out of the box.' In other words, he took what he preached and brought it out into the streets on a level everyone could understand."

But he faced challenges. One of the early controversies, once Dante started to preach, was his use of the word "Amen." He liked to pepper his sermons with "Amens," a common way in some churches to ask people if they were tracking with what the preacher said. He would ask church members to respond to certain things by saying, "Amen!" But early on, some people were concerned that his use of the word was too Pentecostal and part of a looser preaching style than the CRC promoted. It was suggested that he not solicit "Amens" from the pulpit. Heeding the concern, Dante worked to keep "Amens" at a minimum, but it was hard. It was part of who he was.

"In my new Christian life, I attended a church where 'Amens' would ring out constantly to help encourage the preacher. He would preach better and shorter when they encouraged him with their 'Amens,'" he said.

To Dante, Amen, on a higher level, also meant that everything was to be done for the glory of God. The word kept popping from his mouth, because glorifying God was what he believed his life and his work as a minister should be all about. Eventually, the people got used to it and even started calling out "Amens" on their own.

Looking back on his early days at Madison, Dante recalls that he had a sense that the church might actually start to grow. But things were very hard for him. At times he had to pray intently to keep his anger and frustration in check. These were emotions, he knew, that he needed to weed from his heart as best he could because they could get in the way of him doing the Lord's bidding. He eventually learned that, if he let the anger and frustration show, he needed to ask for forgiveness as soon and sincerely as he could from whomever had been the recipient of his unkind words or criticism. Clearly, says his wife, from the start Dante needed to do this—keep a check on himself and turn often to God to help him weather whatever tough situations presented themselves. He needed to keep reminding himself that he wasn't in Harlem anymore.

"Dante experienced a cultural crisis in the first couple of years or so," says Sieplinga. "It was a tough transition and put tremendous pressure on their marriage. He missed New York terribly."

Important from the start, though, was to model racial equality, meaning that Sieplinga shared duties with Dante, calling them the "salt and pepper team." Sieplinga, with a vision for a much more unified future and diverse CRC, knew that people wouldn't take the ministry of the church seriously if he and Dante weren't working as a team.

Rev. James White, Dante's former pastor and by then living in Grand Rapids, met many times with Dante during this period to encourage him in what was a steep, uphill struggle. Early on, despite everyone's best intentions, another problem emerged. Because Sieplinga was ordained, everyone turned to him to solve problems and set direction. Dante was enduring a typical associate pastor situation, a syndrome known to many who serve in secondary roles. "He was the man who picked people up and brought them through," said Dante of Sieplinga. Early on, Dante stayed in the background with no real role to perform. Eventually, he got more frequent and then regular chances to preach, teach, counsel and perform other ministerial tasks.

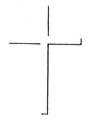

28
OUTREACH

Tuesday night evangelistic trips that church members made through the neighborhood started to draw Dante out. Some 12 people signed up to be part of this team, and Sieplinga and Dante spent time in prayer every week before they went out, encouraging church members to be fearless in sharing their faith with people in the nearby neighborhoods. Dante loved this kind of ministry and was good at it.

Preaching on Sunday, counseling church members, trying to sort through the maze that was the CRC were not easy tasks for the man from New York City. But once he started walking the streets and knocking on doors, he found himself in his element. Dante had a gift for assessing personalities and speaking to people on whatever level that worked best for them. He would approach a home, speak to the occupant and was soon inside, drinking coffee, maybe even nibbling on a little dinner, and talking about the Lord. "One of the most exciting things for me was my love for Jesus and sharing that love with others," said Dante. "I had to be careful, though; I didn't want to go in someone's house and act like a phony. I needed to trust God, knowing that He would lift me up and do the work."

Still, this is what he loved to do. It was what he felt called to do—to tell the story of salvation. When he was held back, it hurt. He felt caged. But when he could speak about God, he felt free. "People grow stale when they're not used," he once told church members who accompanied him on Tuesday nights. "They've just got to be trained to be bold in giving their testimonies, because our neighbors, from the kids on up, think that their greatest need is money. Yet, people are eternally dying out there."

Sieplinga recalls how one time in the winter they were walking down a dark alley on one of those evangelism outreach nights. Suddenly, a pair of mean-looking Doberman Pinchers bounded out of nowhere and, mouths open, headed toward them. Sieplinga was ready to turn the other way and let the growling dogs have their space. But not Dante. He pushed Sieplinga back, raised a hand, saying, "Jesus, you take control of these beasts!" As he spoke, the dogs stopped running, checked out this guy with his arms raised, decided to give up on their attack mode, turned around and walked away. "That was Dante," said Sieplinga. "He wasn't afraid. He gave it over to God."

One of Sieplinga's roles was to serve as a bridge between Dante and the flock at Madison Square. It wasn't always easy, since there were many churchgoers who didn't know what to make of this black Puerto Rican from New York City who commanded dogs to stop in the name of Jesus and who kept infusing "Amens" into his sermons. It was clear Dante enjoyed preaching, but the other aspects of the job didn't seem to interest him too much. "When all was said and done, Dante's call was to be an evangelist, to bring the Good News to people. He brought a spirit that people took in and into their own lives eventually," says Sieplinga.

On the Tuesday evangelism nights, Dante also stopped in the corner bar. He would settle onto a stool, often with Sieplinga and a church member in tow, and start up a conversation with one of the patrons. He didn't small-talk them but got right to the point of why he was there. Even the most hardened boozers seemed to listen. He had a key that opened people up—his genuine interest in them. Here was a guy who was up front, not in your face, but not holding back either, offering simple points on how to approach Jesus. "Dante would share the Gospel with anyone," says Sieplinga. "He would lean over to someone and ask if they had a minute. Usually they would and he started talking." Over time, depending on the drinker's receptivity, Dante honed his pitch down to a one-minute, three-minute, five-minute or 10-minute segment. More than a few of those in the bar eventually found their way to services at Madison Square.

One night a shooting happened right outside the bar as Dante and Sieplinga talked to people inside. When he came out, the bright lights of the cop cars and the ambulance were so familiar to Dante that he felt for a moment like he was back home in New York City. He even thought momentarily of that poor guy whose head he held in the gutter—the guy who was bleeding so much and ended up dying.

29

LESSONS

When he came to Madison Square, Dante was not ordained and needed to take classes at nearby Calvin Theological Seminary. He enjoyed the classes, and yet found them rough going. He deeply appreciated Reformed theology, soaking it up like a sponge. But he began to realize that he also needed another kind of language to help him express the truths being taught in the seminary as well as to develop the best way for him to share the Gospel with others. Providentially, he met a Campus Crusade for Christ missionary named John Veld. Calvin Seminary was one of his areas of ministry. He and Dante struck up a friendship that lasted until Dante died. In the process, Dante learned a few simple and yet extremely effective ways to share his faith. The principles formulated by Campus Crusade founder Bill Bright broke the information down in a structured way that Dante's ADD mind could easily grasp and then "run with," that is, use in whatever context he found himself. Veld didn't ask Dante to be other than he was and worked to simply build on his gifts.

"I liked his enthusiasm," said Veld. "We talked about ministry and how to have a plan you can share with people." Topics they addressed included "How To Be Sure You Are a Christian," "How To Experience God's Love and Forgiveness," and "How To Walk in the Power of the Holy Spirit." Early on, they met weekly at Madison Square but continued meeting for many years at various other spots. While Dante appreciated the intellectual rigor of the seminary, these materials offered him a way to put theology into a framework that fit his learning style. They also gave him a method with which to evangelize and disciple people. That was where his heart was, all the way to the end of his life: evangelism and discipleship.

Other people were helping out as well. Seminary professors reached out to him. Some had him speak in classes about his experiences. In the end, though, the reason Dante succeeded was his own innate ability to take in material, his superb communication skills, and his curious mind. "Dante always wanted to talk things through. I was a listening ear," said Veld. "He never called me John. He called me 'Unc.'"

In a similar vein, Jackie says Dante called her father "Dad" and spoke often to him as well about problems he faced in the ministry. Dante would ask, "Dad, what should I do about this?" The answer: "Preach." Or, Dante would ask, "Dad, what should I do about that?" He always got the same answer: "Preach. Let God's word speak to the situation." They developed a strong bond. For Dante, this was the first time he ever experienced a father's love, and it touched him deeply. In 1996 Dante wrote: "My father was a very critical and abusive man. I do not remember him ever blessing me or encouraging me—ever! He made me feel like a failure—unworthy and judged."

Another measure of Dante's success was the positive approach he always took. He never chastised or talked down to people. "'Thou shalt nots' were not part of his vocabulary," said Veld, who died in 2009. Dante always took time to work with people who were struggling. "He didn't give them a canned solution. He really knew how to love. I was thrilled that he could communicate with such a broad spectrum of people."

Self-knowledge and a willingness to accept and learn from his own shortcomings was key for Dante, and he was helped with this through the Campus Crusade concepts with their practical application of spiritual principles. Equally important, Dante's experience in the streets of New York City and in the prisons helped to guide his gut reactions. Very little surprised or even phased him when it came to the behavior of others. And yet there were always the struggles. Some things got under his skin. Sometimes he was successful at keeping what he saw as his demons at bay; sometimes he wasn't so successful at it.

At one point, he took the Madison Square CRC choir with him to sing at a service in the Ionia prison. As they gathered in the lobby, waiting to be given the OK to enter the prison chapel, some of the choir members started talking and laughing loudly. Some girls sat in the laps of their boyfriends. Dante was embarrassed and upset. When they left that day, he let his anger roll, telling them he would never bring them back with him again. His words stung many choir members. When he realized he had hurt them, he couldn't wait for the Thursday choir rehearsal at church. He went to the rehearsal, humbled himself before them, and asked their forgiveness.

Another example came in the first couple months he was in Grand Rapids. He came out of his house one day to find that someone had stolen his CB radio out of his car. The theft threw him into a rage and he cursed the thieves. He returned to the house and told Jackie he wanted to get a pellet gun and then find and shoot the thieves. She suggested that probably was not a good idea and certainly not how a minister who professed being a Christian should act. Her words stung. They hit home and made him feel guilty. She was right. Still, the anger smoldered. He liked that CB and found it hard to forgive whoever ripped him off.

His unwillingness to let it go didn't start to fade until the following weekend. Someone broke into the church, still located at the time on Lafayette Avenue, and stole the $800 mimeograph machine that they used, among other things, to copy bulletins for the Sunday service. After learning on Sunday morning of the Saturday night theft, he thought of what his wife had said. He went into his office and, instead of daydreaming about pellet guns, he prayed for the thieves, asking God to forgive them and "that they might find peace in their hearts," recalled Dante. He gave the situation over to God. Certain he'd never see the machine again, and well aware that his CB was long gone, he went and taught his 10 a.m. Sunday school class. After class, he returned to the church office and there, just sitting outside, was the mimeograph machine. The thieves had returned it. Dante took an important lesson out of this experience. "I give all the credit to the Lord and the fact that I didn't hold rancor in my heart. When the Lord teaches a lesson, He doesn't fool around."

A young family

30
CHANGED LIVES

Wyvon Gaddie is a residential care counselor at Project Rehab, a drug rehabilitation program in Grand Rapids that celebrated its 40th anniversary in 2008 as the first treatment facility of its kind in West Michigan. Many years ago, he was a resident of Bullock House, a Project Rehab program, where he learned what it would take to transform his life. One of those who helped in this process was Dante Venegas, a tall, good-looking man many people said looked like the well-known singer, Harry Belafonte, a not uncommon occurrence in NYC. Dante went to Bullock House as a chaplain soon after arriving in Grand Rapids in 1978. Gaddie recalls his early days in the facility and how this minister named Dante would show up to talk to people and hold services. "Everyone liked Dante. I remember how they would gather around him when he was done talking," says Gaddie.

"The role Project Rehab played in Dante's life in Grand Rapids was an important one. He volunteered as a Chaplain there for 13 years. He felt comfortable and blessed to be there," says Jackie. "For Dante, being at Project Rehab bridged the gap between his two worlds that seemed so far apart." Friends agree that in the beginning, Dante needed the addicts almost as much as they needed him. They spoke his language. The buttoned-up, hard-to-read culture in Grand Rapids took its toll on him. More than once, it almost drove him to go back East.

But working with people who essentially were not part of the dominant culture gave him an opportunity to relax and be himself around guys such as Wyvon Gaddie, Jerome Burton, and Tommy House. Dante spoke a language they could relate to. Jerome met Dante while in Bullock House. Faith came to him, he said, after hearing Dante open a Bible study with these unusual words:

"Jesus is the hippest dude that ever lived." That got Jerome's attention: "This God he's talking about is for real!!" That realization began a transformation process, ultimately leading to his becoming a CRC pastor.

Former executive director of Project Rehab, Tommy House says that Dante was serving as chaplain at Bullock House when they first met. Addicted to drugs, House almost immediately took to Dante and began attending the classes that he taught on spirituality and its connection with recovery from addiction. "Dante shared some of his challenges as a black Puerto Rican and how he overcame drugs," says House. "Those things that he once lived were so far the opposite of the man I knew." They became long-time friends, especially after House left Bullock House and relapsed. He began getting high again and got to the point in his life where he cared about no one or nothing other than the drugs. Realizing what Tommy was doing to himself, Dante and House's best friend went to see him. "They did an intervention on me. I was struggling with cocaine use and I wanted out," House says.

What struck House, beside the fact that Dante came to his home, was how sincere he was as he recounted, detail by detail, his own drug abuse and then how faith in God, although a long time in coming, helped to turn his life around. Dante stayed in that dark house and with House for as long as it took to get through to him. "I remember that he prayed over me and led me through the sinner's prayer," says House, who started to seriously study the Bible with Dante. "He worked with me for two or three months very closely. He was a solid support."

Dante also spoke to him about how addiction and the Devil were nearly one and the same. The Devil grabbed hold of you and, unless you had the spiritual power of God behind you, would drive you back to addiction, which would lead to insanity, jail and likely unto death. Dante walked him through the things that would happen as he gave his life to the Lord. Drawing on his own personal experience, he laid out the spiritual warfare that House would go through. Dante told him how the Devil worked and would try to entice him back into the drug-taking, coke-snorting lifestyle, especially when he, House, thought he had turned the corner. "I refer to Dante as my spiritual father," says House. "He was foundational in my life. Over the years, he was my advisor when I had important life choices to make."

Despite their closeness, Dante let House find the worship setting that worked best for him. House eventually did this, and by 2010 had followed a call into ministry. Not in the CRC. Wherever he went to church didn't matter because Dante taught him, slowly, carefully and step by step, what he knew to be true: God loves all people—no matter their race, background or beliefs—and longs for a person to willingly give himself or herself freely to Him. Repenting and coming to Him through Jesus is always God's pathway. Getting to that place of release is not easy for some people, as Dante knew. But this was a core of his theology: God is the God of all people and has patience to wait for his children to embrace Him. And one of the crucial parts of Dante's all-embracing story, says House, was his marriage to Jackie and his deep love for his two daughters.

In Dante's approach to ministry with addicts in NYC and later in Grand Rapids, he told them they were in a fierce fight between different warring portions of themselves. An addict could realize that he on his own was weak and needed the strength of God to survive. Or he could follow the allure of the needle. Drugs were powerful. Only God was stronger. No one was going to be able to stay clean on his or her own. Later in life Dante wrote: "My biggest thrill is to see how God uses me with the addicted and the prisoners of life. The responses I witness, not only by those controlled by substances but also by those who administer help, has been a great joy and an honor for me to see."

Dante knew the key role that God played in getting an addict straight. As he sang, preached and counseled at Bullock House, he let the addicts know that he loved them because he had been one of them. With his gift of street poetry, his love-to-laugh personality and an amazing ability to size people up almost immediately, he played an important role in helping maintain a positive spirit at Bullock House, the place where the hardest of the hard in Grand Rapids often landed—broken and bereft.

James Haveman, director of Project Rehab from 1971 to 1979, says he often wonders how someone such as Dante, who had such a hard life in New York City, could be so willing to allow God's hand to touch him and be able to develop such a heart of compassion, especially for addicts. Probably making him so good at what he did was Dante's cold-eyed realism, the realism that is a big part of the Reformed tradition. "He was never surprised at the depth of human degradation and never gave up on his belief that everyone could be saved by God," says Haveman. At the same time, Dante never pretended to be other than he was. He didn't want to be put in a box. In many ways, for the addicts and others, he was a model in persistence and perseverance.

Despite the culture shock, a collision of two completely different worlds, Dante stayed at Madison Square, in the prisons and at Project Rehab to help mend many "broken wings," says Haveman. "His was truly a solid attempt at a multicultural ministry. He taught us how to keep going even when we didn't want to."

31
ORDINATION

The blue-and-red-robed choir from Manhattan CRC traveled by bus from Harlem to join with the choir of Madison Square CRC for the Ordination Service. Together, they belted out spirited songs during the two-hour service on October 18, 1981 at which Dante Venegas was ordained into the ministry. Forty-eight members of the choir had made the trip, and they were busting out with pride to see what was happening with one of their very own Harlem preachers. Their joy, mingled with that of the Madison Square Choir, was clear, loud and infectious. "When I hear that kind of singing," said Sieplinga after the first number, "I could go on all day. And we may do that."

Sara Venegas, Dante's mother, and his two aunts were present. They were excited, overwhelmed and grateful to see how far Dante had come. Over the years, Sara had often told Dante how thankful she was that God had placed Jackie in his life, "an angel sent by God just for you." She deeply loved Jackie and her granddaughters, Andrea and Michele.

After the service, Sara said to Jackie, "Now I can die in peace." She was not ill at the time, but two months later, almost to the day, she suffered a cerebral hemorrhage on a flight to Puerto Rico and died two days later. Dante performed her funeral as he did for many members of his family over the years, including his two aunts, his sister (2002), her two sons (1994, 1995) and his brother (1989). It was very painful and yet he was grateful to play a role in handing them over to God.

Prior to ordination, Dante had to undergo a rather complex and, at that time, unusual, process. Having attended several classes but not enough to graduate from Calvin Seminary, Dante was a special case. Once it was clear that Madison Square wanted to ordain him, Classis Grand Rapids East, the local administrative body of which Madison Square was a member, interviewed Dante and asked him to write a paper to help define his views. In his paper, he wrote that it is only through faith in Jesus "that we have life and are put right with God." He went on to say that things were never as simple as they seemed. Believing in Jesus was much more than a mental or an emotional exercise. One had to follow the truth that Jesus lived and taught. Pastors need to always remember, Dante wrote, that they are themselves sinners and vulnerable to seeking power for its own sake. Quoting Ephesians 6:12 (KJV), he said pastors are in a daily, life-and-death struggle "against the principalities, against powers, against the rulers of the darkness of this world, against spiritual wickedness in high places." The Classis, surprised and pleased by his strong sense of Reformed doctrine as they examined him, passed him on for ordination. Dante was ordained under Article 7 of the Church Order, which allowed for the ordination of people who, without the normal credentials, demonstrated exceptional giftedness for ministry.

Typically, he didn't want to have too much attention placed on the fact that he was probably the first ex-junkie, Black Puerto Rican to be ordained in the Christian Reformed Church. He wanted his life and ministry to exemplify the unity he hoped and prayed would be achieved among people of various cultures and races. "I praise God for the progress, however slow, the denomination has made for blacks and minority leaders. They (the denomination) are putting their foot in the right direction," he told the *Grand Rapids Press* before the ceremony.

Dante loved the research and digging for sermons and papers. He was a well-read man, loved reading the Bible in many versions and deeply enjoyed taking the nuggets he found in Scripture and shining them up to deliver to the people. Still, writing out his sermons in solid Reformed fashion and speaking from the pulpit were hard for him. He always doubted himself and could never quite shake the notion, drilled into him by his father, that he was mediocre and had little that was original to offer people. Was he worthy enough? Could he give sermons that had substance and that presented an important biblical message? In the end, he put aside his doubts and preached, Dante-style. "I was scared, but what was happening was what God wanted to happen. I ended up having extreme fun doing what I did," he said.

Dr. Rod Mulder (d. 2010), a long-time member and leader of Madison Square Church, attended the Ordination service. He had sent a note of encouragement, assuring Dante that he was one of the best preachers he had ever come across. Dante's ordination sermon "was outstanding. It was, of all the good ones you have preached, the best." It was one of the best he had ever heard. In years after, he and Dante exchanged notes of encouragement, building a friendship that endured.

Rev. James White, then a Calvin College sociology professor, spoke at the Ordination, sketching for the people the talents that Dante brought with him to the church. Dante was a leader, but he had an approach that took getting used to. White said he gave credit to the CRC for making room for Dante. Looking back at that time, White says he knew Dante could handle being pastor of a church. The real question was whether the church would fully accept him. "I knew that there were good, forward-looking people in the CRC who would look after him."

Another pastor, Rev. Gordon Negen, charged the congregation with accepting Dante as a pastor and "as a brother." Rev. John Mulder, Jackie's father and Dante's adopted father, was also part of the ceremony and took time to speak of his own father's charge to him 40 years earlier—that is, to handle his responsibilities in a godly manner. Richard Feimster, Deputy Director of Addicts Rehabilitation Center in NYC and a close friend of Dante, also attended. He warned people of what they were in for. "Dante is like a stick of dynamite, and it doesn't take much to get him going, preaching up a storm for the Lord. And sometimes when you least expect it, explosions of exquisite oratory and unexpected suggestions on how to live a full and honest Christian life will occur."

"Congratulations on your ordination into the Holy Ministry," the Rev. John Heinemeier wrote from his Lutheran church in Brooklyn. "You are one of those rare individuals whom I truly believe Ordination has little chance of spoiling. We need more men (and women) in the leadership of the Church like you, Dante."

By the time Dante was ordained, Madison had already grown dramatically from the small handful that had been there when he arrived. The old church no longer served their needs and they purchased a former Presbyterian church on Madison Avenue near a set of railroad tracks. The duo of Dante and Sieplinga kept drawing people who wanted a different kind of church and a more racially integrated form of worship. By now, 225 members belonged to the church. On the day of the ordination, the church was standing room only. Black and white Christians were in the pews, singing and speaking out "Hallelujahs."

With his ordination, Dante was on a par with Sieplinga and they formally launched their co-ministry, hoping that it could serve as an inter- racial model for other churches and for churchgoers to learn from. They had already been doing this, but the ordination put them on an equal footing. "What Dante brought to the church was a passion for sharing the Reformed theology and infusing that great theological framework with a Pentecostal enthusiasm," said Sieplinga. "Dante came to Madison Square and, along with Jackie and the music she played, brought a different style of worship that put us near the forefront of our denomination."

Dante and Sara at his ordination

Three Siblings

32

"WE'VE COME THIS FAR BY FAITH"

Rev. Dante Venegas had hardly been ordained a CRC pastor, and the people had begun settling into their much larger church building, when Rev. Sieplinga announced in the summer of 1982 that he was leaving. In essence, he had done what he had come to do—point Madison Square in the direction of becoming a multicultural church in the denomination. The time was bittersweet, yet festive and even hopeful. "It was one of the great moments in the history of Madison Square when we sadly had to say goodbye to Dave Sieplinga and we read a letter of acceptance from Dave Beelen to become a new pastor at Madison Square," recalls a Madison Square Church council member at the time.

Rev. David Beelen had little idea what he was getting into when he accepted the call to what was his own church. This was his first full-time position as a preacher, and he found that he initially had to lean on Dante for direction. Beelen, who was still Madison Square's pastor in 2011, said it wasn't easy, especially in the first years. He said both he and Dante, along with others in the church, made mistakes and caused one another grief. Yet, what kept him there was Dante's passion for the Gospel, as well as the commitment that church members showed to become "an authentic Christian community."

Church members say that the church survived and began to thrive—counting more than 1,200 members in 2010—because it was always filled with the power of the Holy Spirit. A few still remember the church marching in 1979 from its cramped home on Lafayette Avenue to the new church. On the way there, they carried a banner that succinctly said it all: "The Spirit is on the move at Madison Square" and sang over and over the song, "We've Come This Far by Faith."

That was certainly true as it became clear that Dante and Beelen, despite all of the pitfalls they faced, made a strong show from the start that they were co-pastors. Neither held secrets from the other. They knew that, as they served as a kind of living symbol of racial equality, they had to be honest with one another. Since they came from different cultures, they sometimes just couldn't bridge the gap, but they tried. They shared preaching duties, counseling, baptisms, weddings, and funerals. Through it all, they built a solid relationship. In a way, these friends were also the odd couple. Their worship styles were very different.

Beelen logically planned and seriously gave his sermons. When he preached, he was like a pianist, picking out just the right keys for the symphony he wanted to give. Dante planned his sermons, writing a compilation of notes to support his main points. He would often come to the pulpit singing "I Will Trust in the Lord" and dancing. He would launch into his prepared sermon, but at times found the Spirit inspiring him to go in another direction. He liked to laugh and tell stories appropriate to the sermon. When he preached, he would improvise, like a jazz musician. Some people weren't sure what to think of him, and more than a few left for more staid CRC congregations. He was colloquial, honest, transparent and very serious about handling God's word in a responsible manner. His words were always orthodox. In one sermon, he said, "There was a time in my life when I didn't think I could walk like Jesus. I didn't know then, you know, that it is Jesus that gets inside and makes you walk like Him. Greater is He that is in you than he that is in the world. The Devil is in the world and is no match for you if you have the power of God in you." He said this as he moved and gestured on the stage, locking his eyes with those of the people in the pews.

Jackie recalls how her husband would meditate, talk, pray and study for his sermon all week, trying out ideas, hunches and even conclusions on her, as well as others at the barbershop, in the grocery store or in church meetings. On Saturday nights, once he had it all hashed out, he would write it—generally a compilation of notes and his three main points. "Saturday night became sacred to him. Dante would pray through his sermon, deeply ingesting it into his spirit."

Whenever he was preaching, there was a solid authenticity, even a charismatic quality, to Dante. He was in essence a Pentecostal preacher schooled in and guided by, and eager to talk about, Reformed theology. His sermons were almost a form of verbal jazz, one idea flowing into another but always around a common theme or melody. He moved easily and fluidly, not bound by the pulpit. "He wanted us to take him as he was," says member Donald Huizenga. "He wanted to be himself and be open to letting the Holy Spirit come through freely."

It became clear as the 1980s wore on that Dante hoped the people in the pews would be open to the workings and movement of the Holy Spirit. It also became obvious that Dante was not going to assume the role of the minority pastor who fought hard for racial changes in the city. He wasn't a man to become too involved in causes. He taught racial reconciliation by example. "I didn't come to Madison Square to be a Martin Luther King Jr. I came here to praise the Lord." That statement did not mean that Dante didn't want to see the church integrated. He did, but he wasn't going to force it. He firmly believed that certain ministers, such as Rev. Daughtry and Dr. Martin Luther King Jr., had been called and anointed to that very public type of ministry, while Dante believed that he was led by God to take another approach. "You just be who you are and allow things to happen. You love people and smile," he said. Because of that attitude of not wanting to lead marches or give thunderous speeches, some people wondered if Dante was above the struggle for civil rights, as if he didn't care.

Some people thought he glided through his ministry, trying to remain untouched. That was far from the truth. His heart always ached for equality and harmony between people. His simply was a more subtle and yet very effective ministry. The truth is he touched the untouchables and loved the unlovables, but he rarely spoke about that. He simply went on, knowing that prejudice remained entrenched, in many ways, in the church. "He believed God called him to Madison Square to help bring people into the Kingdom, regardless of their background," says Jackie. "He didn't feel called to be the leader in addressing the issue publicly."

He did get involved, though, in his own way. In the late 1990s and early 2000s, Dante served on a study committee for the state of Michigan relating to health issues being experienced by African-American men. He did this without fanfare, simply took part in a project in which he felt called by God to be involved. In many ways, Dante remained quietly in the background of many people's ministry.

Those involved in what would become the Black and Reformed movement in the CRC would lovingly refer to him, even after his death, as their Bishop. Quietly, he helped start the group, but then faded back. His was the hand that guided people from a spot in the background. "Dante was an inspiration for many of us. He was one of the first people of color to enter and then remain in the CRC," says Rev. Bob Price, one of the leaders of the Black and Reformed movement. "Brother Dante persevered. I know it was not easy for him. There was so much he could not say or do."

Nonetheless, he did serve on race relations committees, attended and spoke at conferences, and served as an ethnic advisor to the church's main administrative body known as the Synod. He didn't speak often in meetings, and frequently sat in his chair and doodled, which actually helped his ADD mind to concentrate. But he was listening. He was aware. He knew how hard it was going to be if lasting change in the area of race relations was ever to emerge and solidify in the church. For Dante and Dave Beelen, race was often on their minds but they didn't make a major fuss over it. They functioned fairly well as a team. Dave could eloquently speak the common language of the CRC, while Dante used it as a springboard to shake things up.

In the early days and even into their later ministry, says Beelen, they would head to the prison in Ionia for an early Sunday service before heading back to Madison. As he watched Dante preaching and interacting with the inmates, he recalls how Dante had the guys "eating out of his hand"—so effective that he was probably one of the best prison preachers in Michigan. Dante kept Dave at his side, and Beelen even remembers how Dante would occasionally give some harsh advice. Once after Dave listened to a drug addict pour out his woes and then prayed with the man, Dante said that at times he was too nice. Dave needed to realize what cons addicts could be and that soft-pedaling the Gospel would hurt rather than help the addict. "I think you're frustrating God's will for that guy's life," Dante told him. "Those struggling with addiction really need to hit the wall and hear God's voice. By being so kind to him, you softened God's disciplining voice in his life. They have to face up to their addiction." Dante taught him how and when to mete out tough love—a type of love born out of his own experiences in New York City.

But they also had fun. Beelen recalls how, when riding in a car together, Dante would sometimes break out in singing a song from a TV cop program that was then popular. In no time, the two of them briefly entered a fantasy world, pretending to be undercover police officers in the Bronx, driving along on the lookout for drug dealers. Dante laughingly referred to him and Dave as "partners in grime." Dave credits Dante with helping to underscore for him the value of using humor in ministry. Without it, he could lose those who were listening to him.

33
PASTOR DANTE AND PASTOR DAVE

Pastor Dante and Pastor Dave, the names used by their parishioners, worked off one another in church with their different personalities and preaching styles. Together, they drew people to Madison. What one preacher lacked, the other seemed to have, and they genuinely showed that they liked and respected one another. Dave was quiet and thoughtful and wry in his humor. He knew the rudiments of his faith and preached it. Dante was looser, bold, an extrovert with an incredible gift of humor and laughter. He, too, knew the rudiments of his faith and preached it. Tension may have smoldered at times below the surface between them, as it does in many relationships, but they showed a common front. "You and Dave are such a good team together in so many ways," a parishioner wrote. "Probably what blesses me most is how you complement each other. Your testimony of faith is so strong and clear from both of you with your very different personalities."

Not too long into their ministry, they realized that the type and number of people showing up on Sundays was starting to change. People from group homes were being brought to church in wheelchairs; tough-looking teens from area rehab facilities were showing up; street people were coming, as was a younger crowd of college students. Addicts from Project Rehab were there as well, mixing with the more traditional members who had been at Madison for years and had seen the church expand from being simply a chapel to a full-fledged operation. This meant Sunday School classes were being expanded, care groups were being formed, choirs begun, activities for teens were growing, and the church began to find itself packed and busy from morning until night with various events, meetings and gatherings. Lay people began to take on more responsibilities, outreach to youth took on special meaning, and the church sanctuary itself became a central place for prayer and healing, open to people in the neighborhood as well as members. Soon, they needed three services on Sunday mornings to accommodate the growth.

Perhaps the most crucial element leading to the growth was the sweeping evangelistic vision that both Dante and Beelen shared for their community. "No longer was it possible to offer a Jesus salvation that refused to come to grips with social injustices," says Rev. Don Griffioen, one of the members back then. Although the church members at Madison were serious about their vision for outreach, they also began to realize that what they wanted to do was not easy, certainly was not simple, and would have to be done in a style that best fit the church and the people to whom they were reaching out.

Dante and Dave would travel once a month to sit on the beach of Lake Michigan at Grand Haven, about 35 miles west of Grand Rapids, to plan the next month's sermons and classes to be offered. Beelen, an avid outdoorsman, appreciated being able to show Dante this part of Michigan. Dante was, of course, familiar with the harbor of New York City, a busy place filled with boats and barges and other types of water traffic. But watching this water stretch as far as the eye could see was another experience altogether. Dante loved it—the expansive sky, the sounds of birds, the lapping of the waves on sand, the carpet of water rolling in from Wisconsin. As for Dave, he always felt Dante was right there with him, paying attention, asking the Lord to bless their relationship and ministry together.

The preachers would bring their Bibles and ideas and would talk for hours, rehashing how things had been going and setting a schedule for the coming weeks. Given his rather free-flowing nature, Dante spoke aloud, jumping from subject to subject, often lyrically, quoting poets he had read and Bible verses he had memorized and loved, allowing Dave to take notes when he wasn't talking. Often, Dante was searching for the right words he would use from the pulpit.

"Words, and the right words, mattered a great deal to Dante," says Pastor Reggie Smith, pastor of Roosevelt Park Community Church, and one of the pastors Dante mentored over the years. "He especially felt that the Word of God, if preached right, had the power to change lives. And he was a living example. He gave me and so many others hope."

In those times on the Lake Michigan beach, Dante and Dave discussed the political ebb and flow of their growing congregation. They knew, almost without saying it, that they were on to something special. When Dante arrived at Madison Square, membership was low, but in a few short years, membership grew and hundreds of people showed up for the three morning services. Ardie Burger, chairman of the elders at Madison Square for many years, says Dante drew people in because "he spoke to them where they needed to be spoken to, and he didn't mind stepping on anyone's toes." Madison seemed to be growing on its own, and yet it required guidance and administration. Dante supported all of the outreach and church ministries, but he was often the idea man and not the nuts and bolts guy who followed through and made things happen. Dante and Dave spoke about this, and it was a source of tension between them at times. As co-pastors, they ought to share all of the duties, but that didn't always happen.

Nonetheless, along with talking about church matters on their many trips to the beach, Dante liked to ask Dave about Michigan with its many lakes, and about the CRC and how he often could not quite understand what people were saying to him or why they asked him so many questions about himself. He knew he was in a denomination trying to change, but it started to become clear at some point that a few of the long-time members of the church, as well as some in CRC's hierarchy, really didn't grasp what Dante was all about. Ultimately, people knew his story of growing up in New York City, but they didn't truly understand what that life, and his amazing conversion, had entailed. He complained to Dave about this, and Beelen tried to reassure him that changes, especially in their conservative denomination, came very slowly. Even so, says Beelen, "Dante was the straw that stirred the drink of multiculturalism in our church. The problem was, political correctness (that is, telling people what they wanted to hear) meant nothing to him." At the same time, though, Dante stuck things out. "He drew racial patience into the church," says Beelen.

34
FROM THE PULPIT

Over the 18 years he was at Madison, Dante touched on almost every subject imaginable from the pulpit. He spoke about what the doctrine of election means in the CRC. He preached about the horrors of hell and how people don't seem to believe in Hades today. He spoke about race relations, about the power of gratitude, about the power and necessity of forgiveness, and sketched some of his own story as to how he was converted while behind bars. But on that topic, at least from the pulpit at Madison, he kept it vague, worried how younger people in the church might react to him talking too specifically about the life he had led.

He preached as well about the church. Once he said, "Madison Square is like a hospital. Everyone comes here for healing of some type of problem or the other. Everyone who joins the church has a broken, sprained, or infected wing, whether they know it or not. Once they are healed by the power of Jesus Christ, they may fly away." Also, "We are blessed to be in a church with ethnic and cultural representation, because if we are willing to look at ourselves, we have an opportunity to be really poor in spirit and then expand our spirit. We will have to wrestle with racial issues glaringly confronting us."

He also preached on the topic of "The Immutability of a Sovereign God," one of his favorite subjects. "In a world of rapid change, in a land of shifting policies and degenerating morals, in a community of constant flux and rotation, one fearfully wonders, 'What is constant?' God is constant, and He makes many promises to those who believe in his sovereignty. These promises were made by God to man, and they reach every part of human life." In this sermon, he got especially animated. He wanted the people to understand the significance of what he was saying. "Saints, whether it is the perfection of promises you are looking for in these times, you are right in seeking them; but these are the best of times and the worst of times. America has prospered materially but has lacked morally." His eyes swept the sanctuary, and he tried with his body language to nail home the important point. He stood straight, jaw set, a hint of challenge in his posture and certainty in his voice: "Listen here, God has already provided a way out for us. He is not going to make another way; there will not be another Christ crucified."

A later sermon was on the topic of walking with God. Dante said that the answer to life's uncertainty and sorrow was to "hold on to the hand of our Papa, even when we are going through some deep waters. Do you know this, Saints? God is always faithful." Touching on his own experience, Dante said, "The Lord has trained me to realize I'll have trials and tribulations. God will be with you, except that you don't know when or how or what time He is going to move. So, Saints, we have to be ready."

In that sermon, he likened God to power steering in a car. Things come so much easier when one has God do the steering. He stretched that image a little further. "The question is, 'Who has the power?' If we want our own power, be careful. The Devil will tell you that you have the power. When you believe that, you jump into the enemy's camp. Satan wants us to be prideful. And it is always pride that comes before what?" he asked people in church, who quickly responded, "a fall." "Yes, indeed, that is the case," Dante said.

Dante often used lessons from his life to illustrate a sermon point. He had learned through experience that the renewing of his mind didn't happen immediately upon his conversion but rather was an ongoing, gradual process. "One day, early in my salvation, I was walking down the street and suddenly found myself unconsciously returning to my old habit of looking into car windows to see if there was anything worth stealing. Suddenly God's voice startled me: 'Why are you looking in those windows? You are resorting to your old way of thinking.' I was not going to steal, but just the idea of looking was the seed for that action. I learned then that only by renewing my mind through God's Word could I have victory over an old habit. And that same truth applies to each one of us."

In 1986, Beelen described what it was like having Dante as his ministry partner. "It is fun," he wrote. "Staff meetings are wild, crazy, funny and serious at the same time—mostly because of Brother Dante. He tells wonderful stories and helps each of us laugh at ourselves. Brother Dante loves the Lord. He is constantly sharing what the Lord has taught him, how the Bible stirs his soul, and how his own sin is being confronted by the Holy Spirit." The two clashed occasionally over worship styles and over administrative duties.

But they always moved forward. When all was said and done, Beelen deeply cared for and admired Dante.

In a letter, Beelen wrote about their sometimes complicated and yet caring relationship. In a tone of self-reflection, he wrote about watching Dante at a Council meeting and how he realized that often Dante had to struggle and fight just to be understood. "I realized how much I loved your determinism to get on with ministry in spite of the fact that you often have a hard going."

35
MEMORIES

Going on 50 years old when he was ordained, Dante was a whirlwind of activity. Besides his preaching, teaching and caring for church members, he continued the work at Ionia prison, where and the outreach at Bullock House. He conducted a Bible study there on Monday mornings and held several groups, during which the residents could speak their minds, in the afternoon. He helped a church member open a halfway house for addicts and alcoholics. He attended seminars on addiction and joined a city task force in the late 1980s that was looking at the crack problem then sweeping through Grand Rapids.

Dante was constantly troubled by how little non-addicts understood of the process of addiction. To many non-drug users, addiction was an issue of self-control and of sin. "I am increasingly concerned over the lack of knowledge within our church about what makes an addict. And that lack," he said, "is reflected by our witness." When people don't understand the dimension of addictions, they could be cruel and unfeeling to those suffering the hunger for drugs or booze. "I often have to deal with new Christians who stumble and stagger because of what they see and hear from people in our body."

Dante had gotten a great deal of schooling in the substance abuse field while working in New York City. After his conversion, he spent a period at James Allen's ARC, but went on, starting in 1968, to take other positions. For a time, he worked to start an ARC rehabilitation facility in New Jersey, which is where he met Sheila Holmes, a member of the church connected with the facility. She would one day go on to become one of the first female African American pastors in the CRC, becoming pastor of Northside Community Church in Paterson, New Jersey. In 2009, she became the first African American woman to serve as a high-ranking official of the CRC Synod, the annual leadership meeting of the church. Dante had been a profound inspiration for her, showing her that a black person might find a place in the CRC. Over time, she has been surprised how quickly people in her denomination have forgotten about Dante and all of the pioneering efforts he made. "He's a minister who left a legacy that we must get to know better," she said. "He led by example. He helped me immensely."

From the late 1980s and early into the 1990s, Dante had to cut back on his work with addicts as he was extremely busy in his role of being a pastor. He loved the interaction with people, preparing sermons, preaching and teaching, especially teaching people how to pray. He showed them that prayer, especially spoken in your own voice from the heart, was an essential part of being a Christian.

At the same time, though, Dante began to struggle with the rules and regulations of the church. He did his best to poke fun at them and ignore them—that is, the need that many felt to conform to an idea that Christianity was straightforward, simple and easy to grasp. You simply had to follow rules and traditions, which seemed to have a richness, life and satisfaction all their own. In some ways it was a club—a club that, when all is said and done, Dante tried to play a role in changing. It is hard to say if he ever had that kind of impact—that is, to change the fairly self-absorbed course of his denomination. There are those, like Rev. James White, who say he ended up failing in the end. The Dutch personality was far too entrenched, often at the subconscious level, to be changed and shepherded into a new world calling for more diversity, at least in the 1980s and 1990s. Dante tried to accept this, always aware that the church was God's and not a church of any one color or ethnic group.

One thing that he could not accept, however, was the frequency with which his last name was turned into a Dutch name. He always addressed the situation. "My name is Venegas, spelled with an 'e'—V**e**negas. It is not spelled 'V**a**negas' or 'Van Egas.' I am Puerto Rican." Sometimes he'd add with a chuckle, "Do I *look* Dutch?"

In those years, the busyness was, at times, a detriment to his prayer life. He couldn't always spend the extended time alone with God that he craved. In February of 1989, for instance, he spoke to community youth at an inner city church and oversaw the Men's Life group that went out witnessing in the neighborhood. In one night alone, they prayed with three people who wanted to receive Christ. He also did a staff devotional at a nearby church, visited people in jail, prepared for two weddings, wound up his work on a committee for the CRC denomination, attended meetings of the Madison Square Redevelopment

Corporation, made hospital visits and helped coordinate a basketball game and pizza party for young adults at church. He also counseled several parishioners, spent hours studying for his sermons, and preached on Sundays.

During this same period, Dante received an award from the Grand Rapids mayor for his role in helping to banish blight, reduce crime, and transform the Madison neighborhood. After his death, the State of Michigan, in a Special Tribute, honored his work. "When the community was under duress with violent crimes and general community dissatisfaction, Rev. Venegas stepped forward to assist in organizing community forums and service centers to address the concerns. To every involvement he brought a unique touch." He also helped lead two neighborhood marches to call attention to the severity of the issues.

In the midst of all of this, Dante touched lives and made a lasting impression on many people who attended or were connected in some way to Madison Square Church. Jackie says she still got letters and cards two and three years after his death from people who said Dante, even though he probably never knew them by name, changed the spiritual course of their lives. He touched people outside the church as well. In 2009, Jackie was invited to attend the Black and Reformed conference held in Grand Rapids. One of the attendees said to her, "Ma'am, I'm honored to meet you. I came up here from Alabama two years ago, so I did not know your husband. But I want you to know that everywhere I go in this city, I hear the name 'Pator Dante' mentioned in the streets. He is still a symbol of hope."

James Haveman says that Dante challenged him and forced him to think differently, and more expansively, about a number of things, especially his own relationship with people of color. "Dante was my inspiration. He challenged me to grow in my faith and social involvement," says Haveman. "Thankfully Madison Square was willing to be open in trying to deal with the issue of racism." Especially, he says, he is grateful that Madison Square didn't force Dante into being a traditional CRC preacher. "They allowed him not to be pressured into the CRC mold."

A former parishioner recalled the time in 1991 when she participated in the annual Hunger Walk that was put on by the Grand Rapids Area Center for Ecumenism. Starting her walk in downtown Grand Rapids, she was eager to keep up a fast pace. She was zipping along, passing people, when someone came up behind and then joined her. It was Dante. As they walked along, they talked about spiritual things and God, and then Dante asked her if she had any special need he could pray for. Dante often taught that people should be specific in their prayers and trust in God to provide. "I sheepishly shared that I needed a kitchen table," she recalls. He asked what kind and she finally told him she would like it to be made of oak. But she only had $100 to spend, not nearly enough for the type she desired. Once they finished the walk, Dante bought her an ice cream cone and prayed for her. "The following week my co-worker asked if by any chance I wanted to buy her kitchen table; she wanted $100 for it. It was oak. It was amazing."

Not all of the stories are happy. One man who attended Madison harassed Dante and his family for years; one winter night he smashed a living room window and another time broke their garage door. He threatened to shoot Dante and to torch his home. He sent them threatening letters that included pictures of guns. His actions terrified Dante's daughters who couldn't understand why he would act this way. This man had psychiatric problems beyond Dante's reach. He had to include him in prayers, asking God to care for this deeply troubled man.

Overall, though, the experience for those who attended the church was positive. Many people carry with them one memory especially. Often before, during or after he spoke, he would spontaneously break out in a song. Many members say Dante singing "I Will Trust in the Lord" was always a moving experience.

> I will trust in the Lord,
> I will trust in the Lord,
> I will trust in the Lord
> Till I die. (Repeat)
>
> I'm gonna treat ev'rybody right . . .
> I'm gonna stay on the battlefield . . .
> I'm gonna stay on my knees and pray . . .
> I will trust in the Lord till I die.

Pastor Dante

36
MENTORING

A significant aspect of Dante's ministry was the often quiet way in which he helped to inspire and mentor a whole generation of younger pastors, a few of whom spoke at his funeral. He was able to do this through the work he did, informally and formally, with young men who were able to bring a taste of newness and a sense of multicultural necessity to their ministries. He worked with them in the halls of Calvin seminary, met with them over lunch, spoke with them at the grocery store, and directly supervised their growth and expansion into ministry—and it was not always the CRC where these people would land. He also worked with many other men who were not going into the ministry; some were recovering addicts; some were new Christians. He was teaching them how to live the Christian life.

In a sermon he gave to celebrate Rev. Dave Sieplinga's 25 years in ministry, Dante gave a good description of what he saw as the pastor's role and a sketch of what he tried to pass on over the years. "The work of a pastor is not purely an administrative office, although some pastors may think and act as if it were. The work of a preacher is one that is ordained and trained by God. He is called by God into this office to bring sinners into the saving knowledge of Jesus Christ." As an illustration of the process one must undergo to become a good preacher, he mentioned how he had a job in New York where the boss asked him to do an inventory of the stock on hand. Dante had never done an inventory before. "He instructed me not to fear making mistakes, and if I got stuck, to please call him." It didn't take long for Dante to realize he had no idea how to do the job right. Fearful that his boss would be mad if he called him for help, Dante tried to do it on his own. Ashamed that he couldn't do it, he finally broke down and called the boss for help. The boss came and carefully showed him how to take on the task, mentioning that in all likelihood, Dante would be able from then on to inventory stock. "I never forgot that lesson. If we are going to do something well, there will be pain, embarrassment, humiliation, etc., but through the process of experience, there will be the ability to do the task well. To do it 'finely.'"

Rev. Sam Cooper, pastor of Community Church of Meadowvale, Mississauga, Ontario, was one of Dante's "disciples" and trained under him at Madison. "Pastor Dante had an intolerance for pretense. He would tell us that following Jesus was costly and hard. He told us that if we were in the ministry long enough, we would suffer for Christ's sake. He knew the battlefield well, from the streets of New York City to the skirmishes in the church." When Cooper was with him, he often felt a sense of freedom and release. As he went about his duties at the church, Cooper kept thinking how Dante's spirit soared above the lethargic spirit that he came across in Grand Rapids. "When one was with Pastor Dante, it was like he, in his own person, could make room for creativity and freedom to flow. His strength was quiet but obvious." At Dante's funeral, Cooper said, "He loved life more than anyone I ever knew."

Rev. Pedro Aviles, a Puerto Rican, also credits Dante with helping to shape his ministry. Aviles is a Chicago-area CRC pastor and a professor of church and ministry leadership at Trinity Christian College in Palos Heights, Illinois. He met Dante in the 1980s when he came to Grand Rapids to check out the CRC and someone took him on a tour of Madison Square Church. "Here was this guy who looked and sounded African American," recalled Aviles at the funeral. "I listened to him praising God and out of nowhere he starts speaking Spanish! He was the connection for me to the church. It was like we were two lost brothers. He was a bridge-builder and gave me the courage to move forward." When Aviles was with him, he felt Dante's attention was on him and not wandering off on something else. "Dante also had a way of looking at life that could see beyond the surface," he said.

Rev. Tom Johnson, a long-time friend of Dante's and pastor of Mt. Bethel Baptist Church in Ridgewood, New Jersey, said Dante sowed seeds of ministry into many people. Johnson and Dante grew up on the streets of the South Bronx and knew many of the same people. However, they didn't really know one another well until years later, after both had been saved, and they spoke after a worship service some place. They compared notes, both entirely amazed that they had been lifted by God from the drug-addicted lives that had been pushing them not only in and out of prison, but aiming them toward premature deaths. At Dante's funeral Johnson preached, "We go back to the streets of the South Bronx together. In those dirty mean streets, the Lord found us.

Who could imagine that God, in Jesus Christ, would be a scavenger and go to the waste places of the earth—where flies don't gather and roaches don't habitat—and pluck out of the earth two men?"

Dante was chased by the police everywhere he went, Johnson said. "In the notorious Forty-second Precinct in the South Bronx, there were two officers in particular who pursued him relentlessly: Sergeants Shatzberg and Kilroy. On one occasion when they apprehended Dante, a smiling Sgt. Kilroy dropped this philosophy on him: 'Well, Danny, it's all a cat and mouse game. We are the cat, you are the mouse.'"

Rev. Johnson says that, for over 30 years, he and Dante got together every June for a weeklong Minister's Conference in Hampton, Virginia. The last time they met there was in 2006. While at these conferences, Johnson said he had to listen to Dante talk about Jackie—how much he loved her and how much she had impacted his life. And how she had stood by him as he transitioned from Spanish Danny to Pastor Dante, even though they went through some difficult times.

His belief, says Johnson, is that Dante loved the ministry and doing it inside the Christian Reformed Church. Certainly, there were setbacks, but he knew that challenges would come. "I knew he felt called to the area, loved the ministry, loved doing evangelism and starting ministries," said Johnson in an interview. "He enjoyed the people. I always believed that he was where he should be. He had a love for the order and structure and the many ministries of the CRC."

Rev. Johnson recalled another experience with Dante. He told this story to Jackie in the fall of 2009 when she traveled to New Jersey for the induction of his son Christopher, Dante's and Jackie's godson, into the Baptist ministry. Johnson first related a little background, reminding Jackie how the Attica prison in upstate New York was taken over in September 1971 by the inmates and has been described as one of the worst prison riots in U.S. history. Many guards were treated inhumanely or killed. "I remember the horror of the event. As things unfolded over those days, there was growing concern in the state about the possibility of this spreading to other prisons," recalled Johnson. He had reason to be worried. On the Sunday during this crisis, Dante and Tom were part of a team that went to Rikers Island to conduct a worship service. They went into the chapel, where there were a couple hundred male prisoners. When they got up on the stage, they noticed there were no guards sitting in their regular seats; usually there were many guards in there, seated in pairs in strategic places. The service began. A bit later, when one of the women team members was singing a solo, it suddenly became eerily quiet in the room. Dante and Tom looked at each other and knew they had to swing into action.

"As we left the stage, we were trying to protect the women, shielding them as we pushed them quickly toward the doors. The prisoners had begun to move toward us, remaining quiet but moving closer and closer in on us. We were very concerned about the women, fearing the inmates might grab them. Edging toward the exit, we talked prison slang as a way of relating to the guys, trying to calm them down and divert their attention from violence. As we reached the doors, the guards opened them and we got out safely. We asked the guards, 'Man, why did you leave us in there by ourselves? Why weren't you in there?'" The guards replied, "We were scared!"

Rev. Johnson says his friend Dante never gave up, remaining a pastor to the end. "There was always some new horizon he was looking at. The Lord was never through with him." Ultimately, by being obedient to God, Dante transcended whatever was going on around him. He stuck with the CRC. "He felt it was healthy and growing, and he felt very serious about the ministries that it was doing," says Johnson.

Pastor Steven Griffin, an undenominational church pastor in Kalamazoo, Michigan at the time of the funeral, spoke at the service. He had attended Madison as a youth. "Pastor Dante was a role model for me. He was a role model for the diversity that should exist in the body of Christ. He even made pastoring look cool. I'm a fruit, produce of Pastor Dante."

Rev. John Nash was one of those whom Dante mentored through a program sponsored by Christian Reformed Home Missions. Nash came to Grand Rapids from Atlanta, Georgia, to intern for two years at an inner-city church in preparation for being sent out to start a church in Atlanta, which he pastored for a number of years. Dante recruited him and several other ministers of color to join the CRC. "I never met anyone who had such compassion and passion for the Gospel," says Nash, currently an Associate Professor in the Religious Studies Dept. at Beulah Heights University in Atlanta. He teaches courses in Old Testament and New Testament as well as a course on Marriage and Family in the General Studies Dept. "Dante was like a prophet or a visionary—like a Jackie Robinson. He was a person who pioneered and had to fight through."

In working with Dante in Grand Rapids, he was always amazed at the people Dante knew in all walks of life and in all kinds of churches. When asked his first impression of Dante when meeting him in 1985, Nash says he was immediately struck: Here indeed was a man of God who acted out of love as he worked with and gave spiritual direction to people. "Dante had such integrity of ministry and of just being a person. He taught us just how hard it was, and how long it would truly take, to have diversity in unity."

37
SABBATICAL

If the story of Dante Venegas could end here, in the late 1980s and early 1990s, at the height of his vitality and influence at Madison Square and the church at large, this would be a tale of serenity and triumph. It would be nice to write about a pastor who retired into a smooth and happy old age, content with what he had done and who was at absolute peace with God. But that is not the story of Dante's final years. Not to take away from his many accomplishments, but Dante's journey, and his connection to that Inferno of suffering, was not over.

Starting in the early 1990s, the problems weren't necessarily new, but they piled up. He had a hard time following all of the changing church regulations and especially abhorred all of the paperwork that it took to keep a large church—Madison in his time grew to 1,500 members—afloat and cruising in the right direction. There were also the constant undercurrents of racism. "There is racism of many kinds—not just white versus black or black versus white. There is class, culture, and ethnic groups who experience racism in many forms," Dante preached. "This church must do something about the racism in our midst."

There was another significant aspect to the difficulties he faced. Dante was trained to believe in the authority of God and that a pastor had been placed by God as the spiritual leader of the church. As a result, he clashed at times with those who wanted to hash out problems in words instead of prayer. Dante wasn't bossy and he didn't want to be the boss. Nonetheless, he did feel called by God to the ministry, believing that the pastor should be the one to lead a church, not out of ego, but out of respect for the office God had created for His church. In the CRC, an individual church is run democratically. It is often decision by consensus, and the pastor is part of this democratic process. But for Dante, the pastor was the leader and should point the way—that is, as long as the pastor and others prayed hard and long for God's wisdom. This aspect of Dante was not well understood. He shied away from conflict, and yet he had deeply held beliefs on how a pastor should lead.

Regardless of his concerns, Dante played a significant role in helping to shape the course of Madison Square's ministry. He did this through example, and not edict. As the 1980s ended and the 1990s began, Dante knew that Madison was at a crucial point: Was it a white church with some people of color, or did it want to be more fully integrated? Not many wanted to talk about this. There were also discussions of worship style at this time. Various groups tended to like things a certain way. There was tension—tension that was probably just growing pains. For Dante, however, these were important issues. He was upset when elders and deacons tried to tell him how to do his job. He says he realized that he was not a "dictator." But he wanted the church Council to let the preachers set the spiritual vision for the church. "It causes too much confusion and frustration the way we operate now," Dante said at one point. "With constantly changing ideas, personnel, and policies, there is great potential for losing the vision as the church grows. It drains me and frequently causes me to feel like quitting."

But he dealt with the tension, although he would have to deal with feelings of rejection and bouts of depression. Few people knew this side of Dante—how much he had overcome and continued to have to face and get over. He laughed a lot, his eyes sparkled, and he seemed happy nearly all of the time, offering a kind word to whomever he saw. But there was that part of him, deep down, a place where that Inferno could still smolder. He had to work hard through prayer, and at times counseling, to conquer.

"He was my spiritual daddy. He helped me come to know Jesus. I worked with him for many years. He was a very good friend," says Ruth Zoodsma, who was on staff at Madison Square. "A lot of people knew him for his fabulous gifts. Yet, they missed who he was. He entered into so many cultures so freely, but few entered into his culture. Only when Pastor Dante was talking to family members, such as his brother Julio, did he seem to really relax and be himself."

But there were those who got to know the relaxed, highly humorous side of Pastor Dante. Ben McKnight, a long-time member of Madison Square, says the thing that impressed him the most about Pastor Dante was his sheer exuberance for life. They became close friends, particularly after McKnight accepted Christ in his life, following a sermon given by Dante on God looking for one righteous man in order to save the city of Sodom. McKnight recalls how Dante ran three laps around the Madison Square gymnasium, whooping and hollering and praising God when he heard from McKnight that he had been saved.

Together, they smuggled junk food into church Council retreats so they could have eating contests. Both of them loved gadgets and exercise equipment, which neither of them ever got around to using, and had contests acquiring the best and most complicated gadgets or pieces of exercise equipment. And then there was the constant laughter between them. "We committed ourselves to a friendship," says McKnight. "He was a good friend and taught us a lot. He was the real deal all around."

Overall, Dante went back and forth on the issue of how much authority a pastor should have. Not being autocratic, the CRC style fit his personality. Yet, on the other hand, he saw both the possibilities and downsides of a model promoting a charismatic, in-charge leader. As was the case in many areas of his life, he felt strongly both ways.

The fallout from one situation, however, proved almost too hard for him to accept. In January 1993, Dante supported a black man to serve as the youth pastor of the church. In fact, the person did get the job, but only after a lengthy and, at times, acrimonious debate at church meetings. Dante was stunned and deeply hurt by some of the things that were said about him during the meetings. But very few people ever knew the depths of his pain and struggle over this incident.

Dante battled with whether he should stay and help the growing church grow more, or take on another kind of ministry. He prayed long and hard, asking God to give him direction. "Some folks may perhaps be wondering about my face," he wrote at this time. "I sometimes appear to be a little down. It's really O.K., but my face just won't respond as quickly as it should. I have been in deep consultation with the Lord here lately, trying desperately to hear clearly the words that He would speak. Please pray for us."

Confused by all he felt and the Hell that he had gone through, Dante decided in April 1993 to ask for a three-month Sabbatical to engage "in creative or professional study activities" that would be "of demonstrable benefit to the ministry of Madison Square." He said he would focus on how to best build and maintain multicultural churches. To that end, he proposed taking a firsthand view of St. John's Lutheran Church, a South Bronx church with a successful focus on education. He would spend time at other New York churches as well and would also visit the Praise Center, the largest Hispanic church in Denver, Colorado. He would take time to read books giving insight into the multicultural church of the future and would attend a minister's institute.

"Pastor Dante will return refreshed and with freshened insights for sermons and outreach programs," he wrote. After receiving his pledge that he would return for at least another three years, the church approved his Sabbatical.

Before he could actually start the Sabbatical, however, he broke from the stress and accumulation of hurts he had experienced. It took three weeks for Dante to be able to pull himself together, through prayer, help from his doctor and the support of his wife. As a result, they did leave for the Sabbatical in June as scheduled. Although unable to do all that he had hoped and planned, he did visit various places and took time out to study and reflect. During the Sabbatical, Dante was refreshed and grew physically, emotionally and spiritually strong again.

When he and Jackie were in New York City, Dante decided to visit his old boss and co-workers at Brookdale Hospital, just to say hello. But he got more than a return greeting. He was actually offered a job by his former employer, a hospital that "highly prized his abilities and giftedness," says Jackie. Doctors there, ironically, had just been talking about Dante, wanting to have him return to direct a start-up HIV/AIDS clinic they were developing and also serve as its chaplain. As much as he hungered to return to his old turf, he turned the offer down, believing that he must keep his promise to Madison that he would serve there for another three years. He had given his word, and he wasn't going to go back on it. "I cannot leave until the Lord releases me," he told them.

Family trip to NYC, 1980s

38
STEPPING DOWN

Dante returned to Madison Square in September 1993 and once again threw himself into the job. Some parishioners had feared he would not return. But within a few weeks, he was as busy as ever. He had four weddings to oversee. He was counseling church members. He got involved at Central High School in a program to keep violence at bay. He took on various speaking assignments at the CRC's Multiethnic Conference. He attended the National Association for Black Evangelicals Conference in Memphis, Tennessee, bringing nearly 20 potential ethnic leaders in the CRC with him.

During this period came the annual October celebration of Pastor Appreciation Day. Although Dante didn't make a big deal out of it, some did. One card represented the sentiments of many. "You are much like our Savior in your gentleness with and love for the children and also in your loving compassion when we need your prayers. We so appreciate your willingness to call sin a sin and to stand against it."

Through it all, though, he was looking into the future. More and more, he saw that his gifts were in one-on-one relationships, in being a chaplain, or in talking to small groups. When he thought of preaching, he began to realize that his voice and gestures were constrained in the CRC. He wanted to let it rip more often than he could from Madison's pulpit—even though he was almost always his animated self, giving sermons steeped in the Bible, Reformed doctrine and using life lessons learned from his own experiences. Essentially, Rev. Don Griffioen says, the CRC wanted to be a multiethnic church, but it just wasn't happening fast enough for Dante.

"We're being overrun by white suburbia. We have to be careful that it doesn't change the focus of our mission," Dante said to the people at Madison.

"Focusing on worship and renewal, there is nothing wrong with that. But we have to look at the other issue. And that is: Who are we? And why are we here? What is the big problem facing the world today? Billy Graham said that is an easy question to answer: Race."

"Often people seem truly unaware that racism is almost in the genes, a sinful and ongoing part of mankind. We are always afraid and critical of the other, and why does that have to be?" asked Dante in that sermon. "It seems as you look at it (racism), worldwide it is an increasing phenomenon and the church of Jesus Christ as a healing agent needs to be in the forefront of reconciliation."

Because Dante had experienced a thorough conversion, he truly felt Jesus provided the grace necessary to address the vast variety that exists in the world and how this variety in all of its multifaceted glory could be brought together and reconciled. The key was each individual's head and heart being transformed into seeing the oneness that could pervade the world. "We must eventually reach the point where we can pray a prayer like this: 'Lord, forgive me for thinking that my way is the right way, and for being unwilling to look at myself to see if there is any wicked way in me. Lord, cleanse me from all unrighteousness.'"

Dante pressed on with his work. Even so, he told Jackie in 1995 that he had lost "the fire in his belly for the work at Madison." A growing awareness that he wanted to move more into his evangelistic calling played into his decision to leave in 1996.

Rev. Dave Beelen, his co-pastor, says there could also be another reason for Dante deciding to leave: Madison Square had become so big. Perhaps most significantly, there was a paradox. Dante's honest, open, and passionate preaching helped draw people to the church. But as the church grew, so did his responsibilities: more meetings, more paperwork, more people to counsel, and even—from a few quarters, in the form of letters and whispered conversations—criticism of how he did his job. "We were cooking along and he was approaching 65 years old," says Beelen. "I think things wore him out." At heart, Dante was an evangelist, a wonderful storyteller, but not an administrator. He was never happier than when he was talking about Jesus. His passion for Christ was contagious. "He sort of became a victim of his own success," says Beelen.

Although Dante was a music lover, artist, writer and voracious reader—of biblical commentaries, of theological books, of books on ministry issues, of poetry, of classic novels, and of the Bible which was always central—he didn't like to be put in a box. His creative impulses took him where they went, flying high into the world of ideas and theology. He didn't like answering the phone, keeping regular office hours, or even planning too far ahead what he would say from the pulpit. He desired to stay close to his muse, his own sense of personal revitalization, not wanting to sway too far from the roots of who he knew he was in his guts. "I think Dante wanted to get back to where he started—working in smaller settings, especially with addicts, as an evangelist," says Beelen.

In some sermons, Dante continued to question the issue of growth, asking if the real power of a church was in its numbers. He tried to keep Madison on course, helping it to grow in the Lord. He believed it was a one-on-one relationship that pastors helped establish and nourish between their members and God that mattered most. "Leaders take note!" he preached in January of 1994, about a year after the building of a large new sanctuary was completed. "Satisfactory buildings and well-organized operations are essential, but getting your people grouped, protected, and relating smoothly with one another is equally vital. Those walls must surely be built, but a true and effective leader makes sure that what happens inside the walls is effective, too. Amen?"

While Dante experienced conflicts over the issue of growth, he clearly wasn't always consistent. On one hand, he seemed to dislike it. On the other hand, he took pride in helping to make it happen. "Our organizational structure must be tightened up," he once said. "I feel we have too many loose ends and that we are still operating with a small church mentality." Madison, he said, had big dreams and a solid future.

The searing search of his heart and soul finally came to an end, leaving Dante with a clear sense of what he had to do. He stepped down from his job at Madison Square in August of 1996, fulfilling his promise of staying on for at least three years following his Sabbatical. In his final sermon, he acknowledged how much the church and its people meant to him. But he also said being co-pastor at Madison Square "was sometimes like being in a crucible." However, his time had come. He wanted to move back to the type of ministry that best suited him. Afterward, a church member came up to him, sobbing, unable to tell him how much he had meant to her for so many years in the mountains and valleys of her life. Dante wiped away her tears and then gave her a hug. "It's gonna be alright, Baby. Everything's going to be all right," he said.

Others also wept. Many offered him well wishes and reflected on how Dante and his wife had played such significant roles in their lives, standing with them in countless times of sorrow and celebrating the victories when they came. One parishioner wrote, "Their love and respect for each other was very obvious." "How can we say 'Thank you' for eighteen years of faithful service to two such precious people?" wrote Madison Square member Don Huizenga in a letter. "However, we trust that you two will sense the thanks that is in all of our hearts as many of us stumble for words." As for Dante's ministry, wrote Huizenga, "Your leadership has made welcome a wide variety of people. Your powerful testimony about the work of God in your life has planted a seed of hope in our lives that the miraculous power of God is able to save us and sanctify us as well. Our denomination has been enriched by your presence."

One parishioner's note powerfully summed up Dante's heart for ministry. "Some years ago, I was going through a very difficult time in my life and had stopped going to church. One day after coming home from work, I was sitting in my living room when my answering machine came on. I heard your voice coming through the speaker, without introduction, lifting me up in prayer to the Lord. I listened and I cried, weeping to hear that I was loved and accepted for who I was. You poured out grace to me on that answering machine. How do I know it was grace? Because you did not admonish me, you did not chastise me for not being at church, you did not ask me for anything. You just gave me grace."

Dante, quick to laugh.

39
FOLLOWING HIS HEART

At the suggestion of members of the community, Dante considered running to be a Grand Rapids City Commissioner after leaving Madison. He was no stranger to local politics. For 14 years, from 1988 to 2002, Dante was a member of the Supervising Agency for the Madison Square Redevelopment Corporation. He loved the work, enjoyed the meetings and thrived on the wide variety of people involved in bringing vitality back to the area that meant a great deal to him. Dante recalled how the neighborhood struck him when he moved to Grand Rapids. It seemed so barren of healthy life, a scourge on the southeastern end of the city. He was pleased that he could play a role in again bringing hope, businesses and needed city services to people in the neighborhood. He would walk the area, a bounce in his step, as he saw apartments go up and bulldozers raze dilapidated storefronts to make way for new businesses and enterprises. He was pleased to see the bar closed.

With his heart for the neighborhood, some felt that he could help the Madison Square Business District even more by being a member of the City Commission. He thought seriously about it but gave up that idea when some critics started complaining he was not black enough to represent that part of the city. He didn't need that kind of grief. Clearly, running for office would be an uphill battle.

Instead, Dante began looking to serve as a chaplain, to return to closer relationships with people. He had always enjoyed witnessing and bringing people into a closer walk with God. He wanted to branch out in a lower-key kind of way. In addition, he was getting older and wanted to spend more time with his wife and daughters and grandchildren. He took deep delight in this.

But he also kept working for God. Over the years, it became clear that one of Dante's greatest gifts was that of discipling others into becoming effective workers in God's kingdom. He did not want to give up mentoring, desiring to build men and women who could be strong in their faith and get into ministry. His influence remained. It had to. Dante was Dante, and he always needed to talk about God.

Following his heart, Dante became Director of Chaplaincy Services at Alternative Directions from 1996 to 1999. Considered a CRC chaplain, he provided counseling to staff and residents of the 24-hour live-in facility for males who were convicted of minor offenses and sentenced to live at the halfway house on South Division Avenue. The probationers listened to Dante's words about giving their lives to a power greater than themselves. He taught them the principles of living a solid Christian life and told them not to give up on church. He wanted them to realize that churches did have hypocrites in them, a frequent accusation by the guys, but they were also home to a great many good people.

In this job, he drew not just on his own experience. He had studied intensively in the Chaplaincy program at Pine Rest, a Christian psychiatric hospital located in Grand Rapids. He received a certification from the Association for Clinical Pastoral Education for the 400 hours of study he undertook in the late 1980s. He was clearly well prepared for the job. "Alternative Directions was great. I was able to relate to those guys," Dante said. "But eventually I was getting tired. Something was wrong with this picture. Somehow, it got to feel old. I was there three years and wanted to go back to church ministry."

40

CITY HOPE

Dante felt led in the fall of 1999 to help start a new church, a joint venture between the Christian Reformed Church and the Reformed Church in America. Called City Hope, the congregation met in an old, inner-city church that had water-stained ceilings, worn carpet and crumbling plaster. For a time, Dante was elated to be back in the job of being pastor of a small congregation. Once again, people were blessed. "He was back in the pulpit and the same as he was at Madison. He was telling people about the Good News," says Sterlon Robinson, known to Pastor Dante as "Boonce." He had attended Madison for many years and his grandmother was "Mama Lu," Dante's adopted mother. He followed Dante to City Hope. "He was still full of the Holy Spirit," recalls Robinson, who was only six years old when he first met Dante. "I talked to him one day after a service and we prayed. I remember how in that particular moment, the power of the Holy Spirit became even more real to me."

Dante asked him to join the church, hoping he could help as City Hope found its direction. Sterlon says he has always felt bad for not taking Dante up on his offer. Married with three children, he couldn't make the commitment. He then saw how Dante struggled with his fellow pastors. They seemed to disagree over which direction to take City Hope.

Dante was helped in the new ministry by Rev. John Matias, then the associate director of Multicultural Affairs at Calvin College in Grand Rapids. For various reasons, says Matias, Dante struggled in the church. City Hope started to show some of the tensions that he had faced at Madison. On a deeper level, maybe he was troubled that he was seen simply as a black pastor at a new church and that "he was never able to celebrate his Puerto Ricanness." In a broad way, Dante never stopped being a minister seeking unity. "He hung in there until his death."

City Hope began with high spirits and optimism. Dante once again knocked on doors of people in the neighborhood, asking if he could pray for them. He also loved and cared for the parishioners. Although the ministry wasn't a good fit for Dante, he remained there until February 2002. "My partners wanted to do things differently than I did. They wanted to do what they wanted to do," Dante said.

The church was still in existence in 2011 and had a range of ministries, implying that the idea of locating there was good, but the early execution might have been a bit lacking. As for Sterlon Robinson, Dante always remained an inspiration, a father figure, but there was something else as well. "He didn't just walk by and say, 'Have a good day,' but he would stop and try to make your life better. He was in touch with his powerful spiritual self. He was just like Jesus was in his love for and non-judgmental attitude toward people."

From City Hope, Dante still wasn't ready to retire from ministry. He took a job as a part-time chaplain at Health Intervention Services (HIS) in Grand Rapids, also serving as needed as a Spanish translator between patients and caregivers. "He was genuine, compassionate, direct but loving," says Sylvia Daining, executive director of HIS. "He would stay for hours with patients, simply sitting at their sides. He would talk with them, listen intently to their stories and tell them about healing that was eternal. We were so grateful to have him." Dante recalled that it was through his reliance on God that he could remain so close to the patients, especially those suffering great pain, and keep on loving them, even when it seemed they had stopped loving themselves. Being in that environment, he heard many stories from patients about the struggles they experienced paying for health care. When this happened, Dante said, he wanted to break a hole in the roof and bring Jesus down so he could bring healing. Jesus never sent a bill; his services were there for the asking. As he looked into wrinkled, aging faces and saw how what he said touched them, he knew that God was real and at work: "You don't love with your own strength. You have to love with God's strength. You can't do it alone."

Dante received many offers to preach in churches and spent many Sundays filling other pastor's pulpits. One Father's Day, he preached that it was a great day to honor men "who have had memorable and significant relationships with their fathers. Those who have learned to become productive adults through a healthy father/son relationship are free to live responsibly in their communities, making impressive and acceptable contributions to it. Too many of us however, including me, experience negative relationships with our fathers, and as a result, we repeat the sins of our fathers—getting into addiction, becoming abusers, divorcing."

Dr. Joseph Horak, a psychologist who counseled Dante for several years, says it took a great deal of prayer, talk and emotional turmoil for Dante to accept and then really start to heal from the often abusive, and always complex, relationship he had with his father. While the hurt and loss lingered, he was able to move on and to forgive his father. The forgiveness didn't come easy, but it allowed him to finally be free of his father's power over him. Of his immediate family, in fact, he was the only one able to do so—to see any value in his father and be able to forgive him. Dante attributed his ability to heal in part to the work he did with Horak.

But Dante also attributed his ability to move on from a terrible childhood to God's supreme grace. In that Father's Day sermon, Dante recalled his own salvation. "While confined in that small cell in Bronx County Jail, I confessed all of my known sins and asked 'Whom It May Concern' for forgiveness. I was dramatically filled with the Holy Spirit and lifted spiritually from my circumstances." In another sermon, he spoke about joy. "Distress must not be viewed as if it would last forever. It is not the end, but only a means to an end. At the moment when God turns us from our captivity, the heart turns from its sorrow; when He fills us with grace, we are filled with gratitude. And Gratitude gives birth to Joy!"

Dr. Horak says that Dante was "an addict who committed crimes to support his habit. He did not have a criminal mind. He did what addicts do." Horak also said in an interview that the key to Dante's ability to overcome his violent childhood, drug addiction, prison, and then become a much-loved pastor, was that "he stayed in touch with his humanity and that kept him grounded and real. This was the key to his spirit of humility."

City Hope

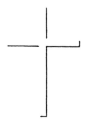

41
THREATENING CALLS

In February of 2000, Dante came home from attending a revival service featuring the popular Texas preacher, Bishop T. D. Jakes. It was about 11 p.m., so he was shocked to see two official-looking men sitting at the table with his wife. "When they introduced themselves and told him they were from the FBI, I watched his face and saw a look in his eyes that I had never seen before. He immediately took control of the situation by greeting them and shaking their hands; then he asked why they were there," says Jackie.

Seeing the agents reminded Dante of the terrible day way back in 1957 when he was walking down the street and suddenly found himself accompanied by two men, each one grabbing an arm. "Dante Venegas, we are the FBI and you're under arrest." Trying to stay calm on that New York City street, Dante laughed nervously and asked, "How did you find me?" They pulled out a wad of checks that included every check he had forged. Caught red-handed, he agreed that he indeed was Dante Alighieri Venegas and that he was the one responsible for stealing and forging all those checks. He was sentenced to Lewisburg Federal Penitentiary for three years. It was there that he discovered that his best friend had snitched on him, helping the FBI find him.

On that night in Grand Rapids 43 years later, Dante again kept his cool as Jackie assured him that everything was all right. "I told him about the threatening phone calls we had begun receiving after he left for the revival. A former parishioner who had harassed our family for years in the 1980s had called. When I answered and heard his voice, I recognized it immediately."

The man called repeatedly, making unspeakable threats against both Dante and Jackie as well as the President of the United States. Since he called so often to utter his threats, Jackie allowed the answering machine to record the calls.

Unable to determine where the man was calling from, she called the police. An officer came out and took a report. Very concerned for Jackie's safety, he left her with specific instructions of what to do in case the man was in Grand Rapids and came to the home.

"Twenty minutes after he left, I received a call from the FBI telling me that U.S. Secret Service agents would have to come and interview me. A couple of hours later, two local agents came. So when Dante arrived home, they had already listened to the messages, totaling about 32 minutes," says Jackie. The agents explained that the messages were indeed extremely disturbing for the family, but that they were involved because of the threat to the President.

"These are exactly the kind of guys that kill presidents," one of the Secret Service agents told Jackie and Dante.

"The agents recorded the messages as they gathered more information from us. They left our home about 1 a.m.," says Jackie. "Early the next morning we received a call. They had picked up the phone caller in Texas about 3 a.m. His name was on the FBI Watch List."

42
RESILIENCE

Despite the intrusion of the FBI and the old memories that the unexpected encounter brought up, Dante persevered. In his mind, jails and the FBI and rehab joints were well behind him. Although he was then starting to feel the wear and tear, the wrenching reality of the many difficulties he had faced over the years, Dante didn't give up. He had begun to feel very tired and sapped of energy. But he shouldered through the physical difficulties. In his mind, he had faced many types of flamethrowers, fire aimed at him from many directions, trying to devastate him over the years. He faced those fires, those challenges, though, and while singed and scarred, always emerged intact. Until the end, he availed himself of God's refreshing, abundant grace.

Dave Beelen says he was always amazed at Dante's resilience. Roadblocks that would have turned other men around didn't really faze him. Dante found ways to get around them, especially in the denomination he served for nearly 29 years. "I can't imagine anyone in the CRC who broke down more barriers, especially racial ones, by the way they lived than Dante," says Beelen. "He could relate to the rich as well as someone who was an addict and high at the time they talked." Dante was a groundbreaker who stayed out of the limelight.

Wanting his example to show the way, Dante didn't push very hard through official channels to further the cause of race relations in the CRC, but he had his opinions. In 2004, the CRC held its biannual Multiethnic Conference (MEC) that is a forum in which minorities could speak about the problems and challenges they faced in a predominately white denomination. Having attended other, similar forums over the years, Dante knew what to expect and wanted to go. But he wasn't feeling well enough to attend.

Instead, he took the opportunity to write down his thoughts for the conference leaders, offering advice, sketching his approach. He believed that prejudice and racism were sins and, therefore, issues of the heart. "The response to racism," he wrote, "should be more pastoral than political. Perhaps the conference could attempt to be more intentionally inclusive and tolerant of the denomination and have more focus on the person of Jesus Christ and the Holy Spirit." He suggested they use the conference to educate people about how Christ was the healer and less to allow it to become a forum to air grievances. "Balance, tolerance, humility and forgiveness are good words to keep in mind on all sides as MEC plans for future conferences. Keep in mind that racism can't be eradicated through angry outbursts or pointing of fingers. Always, one must work with God to remove racism from one's own heart. Freedom doesn't come easy."

Dante was always trying to bring people together. Wherever there was brokenness in any type of relationship, his desire was for reconciliation. In a 2001 sermon on reconciliation, he ended with these words.

"Once we have discovered the facts—who, when and where—God calls us into Gethsemane. Gethsemane is that place of prayer where Jesus laid aside His righteousness and became all that we are. We are called to lay aside all our righteousness—until it is no longer important whether we or the other guy is right or wrong. As Jesus became sin, so we need to say, 'Lord, make me to know my sin, and so identify me with the sin of all mankind that I may know my oneness with my brother at the foot of the cross.'

"We cannot get to the cross except by going through Gethsemane. If prayer for death of sin on the cross has been expressed many times, and yet that old pattern continues to operate, we need to return to base one and examine whether fullness or forgiveness of self and God has been accomplished. This occurs when we identify our sin and wrestle our emotions away from attachment to the old way. Otherwise, we will, in effect, snatch our old way off the cross before Jesus cries out, 'It is finished. Father, forgive them.'"

Sketch in ink by Dante

43
THE DIAGNOSIS

Dante was still serving part-time as the chaplain at HIS in January 2005 when he learned that the long-time weariness and discomfort he had been trying to ignore came from something more sinister than age. He learned that he was suffering from non-Hodgkin's Lymphoma, a tough cancer to beat. Tears flowed in Dante's family as they came to grips with the diagnosis, and especially the daunting prospect of the grueling treatment that doctors described. He had the type of cancer that floated through the body and could not be easily isolated and destroyed. Doctors had to bombard him, again and again, with drugs.

The disease and the chemotherapy treatment took a toll on him. His hair disappeared for a long time; he sometimes found it hard to maintain his normally upbeat mood, and unexplained bruises kept appearing on his body. Dante did his best to take this disease in stride. God had given him many good things, and now came cancer. "I don't want to be sick, I don't want to die," he wrote in a letter. "I don't want to see or experience personal suffering. I want to live and proclaim the works of the Lord." Battling cancer, Dante found he had to speak to others about the disease, since they cared for him, and he wanted them to know what he was going through. "Whenever I mention the disease that has come upon me, some are stunned into disbelief, some weep, and others don't know what to say. Some offer words which I know are well-intentioned and meant to comfort me but are spoken from an uninformed or misunderstanding of the true Word of God. Jesus, after all, underwent his own time of suffering and rose again. He paid the price for mankind's sin. When you keep that in mind, you can give thanks in all circumstances."

During his treatment for cancer, Dante reflected in writing about his life in his journal and how he was "'Hispanic by birth, Black by choice, and Christian by Providence.' When I look back, I see the hand of God was on me." The mixture of his early years—born and growing up in Spanish Harlem and then moving to the mostly black neighborhood in the Bronx—he considered a "training ground for becoming multicultural with no hidden agendas. In Christ I found life and light that enabled me to relate to everyone." As Dante reflected hard on what had motivated and driven him during his many years of ministry, the word "agenda" came back again. "As an ex-addict and ex-con, I'm supposed to have hidden agendas. I don't and that blows people away. My only agenda is that souls be saved and discipled. And that blows people's minds. That's what God called me to do. He called me to be a mind-blower!"

One of the young men Dante had mentored in prison wrote him a letter around this time. He and Jackie had gone many times to visit him in prison. Even in his sickness, Dante continued to visit this young man, sentenced to life for murder. In the letter, he wrote to Dante: "I pray that you stay healthy and get better. I may be a little down and out now but you taught me well; so you know I will do like Paul and shake it off. You're the best father figure a guy could ever have and I love you with my all."

Letters such as this lifted his spirits. But even as his cancer went into remission, pain continued to wrack his body. Still, he kept his focus on God. His relationship with the Lord deepened. He didn't blast God for his problems. Rather, he asked God to stay close and, whenever possible, allow him some relief and an ability to have fun, especially with his family. God was no distant being. God was Dante's comrade and comfort. God was his beginning and his end.

The Cancer Journey

44
THE PAST INTRUDES

Dante and Jackie flew to Vancouver, British Columbia, in December 2005 to spend the holidays with their children and grandchildren. Without trouble, they seemed to be clearing customs, but then a gruff immigration officer stepped up and ordered them into the nearby office. The couple had no idea what they were about to undergo. Once again, Dante's criminal past intruded. Apparently, Canadian officials had done some checking before the plane landed and discovered that this ailing pastor with cancer had been in jail and prison several times 40, even 50, years before. "You certainly have been a busy boy," the official said to Dante while demanding that he and Jackie surrender their passports. The demeaning tone in the officer's voice deeply humiliated and upset Dante. He and Jackie were shocked and frightened but knew it was not wise to make any kind of reaction. Without their passports, they had no rights. It seemed unfair: post 9-11 rules and regulations had caught up with Dante.

They waited quietly in a small room, feeling the tension mount. They were not allowed to leave the room to get something to eat or drink, and they were escorted to the restroom by a guard. Jackie got on her cell phone to tell their daughter, Andrea, what was happening and to ask them to pray and, if possible, get others to pray for them as well. She contacted someone and a prayer chain was started immediately.

Over the next three hours, the agent returned twice with the same message: Dante's criminal record could deny him entrance to Canada. Stunned, the couple sat there, feeling helpless, wondering how things that happened so long ago could intrude so forcefully now. When the officer returned for the third time, his demeanor was stiff and formal, and he was carrying the full weight of the Canadian law on his shoulders. "He announced that we were not going to be allowed to enter the country or see our children and grandchildren, even for a half hour," Jackie recalls. "They were preparing a plane, and within the hour, they would fly us to the first relatively close airport available in the U.S. If no airport was available, they would put us on a bus and drop us off just over the border. From there, we were on our own to find a way to get back home."

Hearing this, Dante staggered and quickly turned ashen. Jackie began sobbing uncontrollably. The officer then told her that she could enter the country. But she refused, informing him that Dante was sick with cancer and she needed to be with him. She brought out papers written by his doctor, describing his condition. When the immigration officer heard what she had to say and read the documents, his personality softened a bit. He became more of an advocate for them.

Dante began struggling for breath in his weakened and crestfallen state, and Jackie rushed to his side. When the officer saw this, he asked Dante to sit down and waited for Jackie to finish assisting him. The officer told them that Canada had a "compassion" provision to allow people in and that he would do what he could to help them. "I guess it's safe to assume that a 72-year-old man dying from cancer is not coming to Canada for a crime spree," the officer said to Jackie in a soft but slightly disparaging tone. Following that, however, he treated her respectfully as they filled out the necessary paperwork. When finally completed, he again took it to his boss. "When the final OK for us to enter came 45 minutes later, he stapled a special permit into Dante's passport," says Jackie. "We had to pay $200 and we left with gratitude to God in our hearts for being free. It didn't even matter to then find out that our luggage was in Houston. We were free!"

In order to remove the impediment of his criminal record from his inability to get into Canada, Dante had to fill out an "Application for Determination of Rehabilitation." In it he wrote that from May of 1966 until then, May 2006, "I have lived a drug-free, crime-free life. I thank God for my changed life, and humbly request that I be granted permission to enter Canada as a changed person. I desire to visit my children and grandchildren who presently live there."

Dante had to request from friends and colleagues letters attesting to his recovery; they had to accompany his application. In many ways, though, they are yet another testimony to what Dante and his ministry had meant to so many people over that 40-year period. James Allen, Executive Director of ARC, informed authorities that Dante came through the program for treatment in the early 1960s and then later was on the staff. "We heartily stand behind Rev. Venegas in attesting to over 40 years of sobriety and deem him to be rehabilitated. He stands as a symbol of hope to those bound by addictions," Allen wrote.

Carol Visser Wolf, a clinical psychologist in California, told Canadian immigration authorities that she had never met "a more loving, gregarious, caring, decent man. He is a man whose heart is good, and demonstrates this daily in his behavior, attitude, and acts of kindness." Rev. Jack Kooreman, pastor of Grace CRC in Grand Rapids, informed authorities that he was well aware of Dante's criminal past, riddled with addiction. "It's not something he hides but freely shares with anyone who will listen. He is a man of great integrity and faith. He has been an inspiration to me and so very many others. He is known in Grand Rapids as an important Christian leader."

Among those providing references was Joel Huyser, a former practicing attorney who is now a missionary for the CRC in Central America. He, too, vouched for Dante. In a separate interview, he had several other things to say about him. Joel had served on the Madison Square Church council during much of the time that Dante served as pastor. Dante hated meetings of almost any kind, partly because he often felt misunderstood. While many people in the meetings tended to think through an issue **before** talking, Dante thought through an issue **by** talking. He might start in one place and end up in another, which baffled some people. "The decision-making process is very different in Dante's culture than in ours. We tend to think things through. In Dante's culture, they work it out verbally. Also, Dante was a product of the jazz culture. As in jazz, he was always trying to balance himself with the opposite," says Huyser. "Maybe that is why he married Jackie, who could anchor him. In addition, he needed the straight, systematic Reformed theology to ground him. He attended a Pentecostal church after his conversion and carried much of its intuitive, spontaneous qualities with him into the CRC."

Huyser was always amazed at how well Dante crossed cultural barriers. He didn't do this because he thought it was a good idea. He did it because of who he was. "This is an essential part of the story. It is one of the questions raised by his life. How was it that this former addict had such a tremendous influence on the church, an influence that endures to today? Dante was probably the most color-blind person one would ever meet. One of the ironies is that, though many tried, few others were able to cross that racial barrier."

In fact, Dante was one of the racial pioneers in his church and denomination. It is not hyperbole, says Huyser, to say that people like Dante helped break cultural barriers and pave the way for racial change in the church as well as in society. Dante was a man who always moved forward and didn't stew in his disappointments. He was in many ways an unsung hero, "a reluctant warrior on racial issues. This was not because he did not have convictions," says Huyser. "It was because he didn't want anything to distract from his personal calling from God, which was first and foremost to be an evangelist. As an evangelist, Dante was sensitive to the deep spiritual hunger in all sorts of people. He became a living example of what it truly means to cross racial and cultural barriers. Dante had something special and unique. He was able to communicate a freshness and an aliveness to the Gospel that a lot of people had never experienced."

It is also important to note that, despite some struggles with his denomination, Dante was not unrecognized. Over the years, he served on several denominational committees. For nine years, he served on the Board of Trustees for Kuyper College in Grand Rapids, a ministry-focused Christian leadership college with a Reformed worldview. He was chosen as the headline speaker for the first worship service in which Synod and the Multiethnic Conference formally joined together. His face was also included in the painting called "Grace Through Every Generation," which was done as part of the 150-year celebration of the CRC in 2007. And at the Multiethnic Conference in June 2011, Dante was honored with a posthumous award as a Diversity Champion for his important role in race relations in the CRC.

After Dante's death, Rev. Lou Tamminga, the denomination's long-time pastor to missionaries, wrote Jackie. "I remember Dante for his uniqueness: the visionaire, his initiatives, his courageous concern for the ill-treated, and his consistent honesty, which was sometimes uncomfortable for his friends. Dante was a good and necessary influence on the CRC. We thank God for him and his ministries."

One year after Dante's death, Andrea and her sons came upon this scene while hiking in Hornby Island, British Columbia. Their first response: "That's what Papa said!"

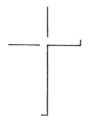

45
"I KNOW THE LORD IS HEALING ME"

Dante's cancer was insidious. He believed thoroughly in the healing power of God, but he also knew that man is a fragile creature and that death comes to us all. For a period, he was in the limbo that cancer provides between life and death. But limbo was not where he was headed. The situation he faced could be summed up by a section of Dante's *Divine Comedy*, a classic he read, often seeing the parallels with his own life. In this case, it was glimpses of Heaven.

> In that heaven where His radiance most glows
> was I, and saw things he who thence returns
> no knowledge has, nor power to disclose.
>
> *Paradiso*, "Canto I"

Dante knew Heaven was coming closer. But he must first continue his journey. Despite the frequent ups and downs following chemotherapy treatment, he held onto his faith. However, he was in pain, even after taking potent painkillers. His moods were at times mercurial. Frustration would erupt, often directed at members of his family. This upset him greatly, but his body was now at the mercy of the disease. At times his mind seemed a bit addled and he forgot things. His wife stayed at his side as the cancer began to take up more and more of his life. He tried to work, but the terrible, almost unimaginable, weariness and pain that overtook him often kept him from his work at HIS.

With an increasing level of pain for which there was no explanation, Dante might be bed-ridden for days, and then he would rally. In September 2006, about seven months before he died, Dante scribbled a few thoughts on the drugs he had to take to keep the pain at bay. He knew drugs. He once loved and lived for them. But no longer. They were simply pills he had to take to maintain himself. He could look beyond those pills, their haze and false promises, to a remedy that was eternal.

Over the years, many had told Dante that his religion was a crutch and that he had traded in his addiction to drugs for an addiction to religion. Often these barbs were spoken in a prideful and judgmental tone: "I don't need a crutch and to have one is a sign of weakness." This criticism didn't rankle Dante. "I cop to the indictment," he would reply. "I know I'm powerless in my own strength to live the Christian life, and that only through Jesus living in me can I live this life. Give me this crutch any day!"

Dante and Jackie needed to make it to seemingly endless doctor's appointments. As the physicians did their tests and probes, Dante tried to keep up a good humor, although the unrelenting pain greatly impacted their lives. But he held on to hope: "I know the Lord is healing me—either a miraculous healing on earth or my eternal healing in heaven."

"During this journey," Jackie wrote in an email, "we have experienced a great cloud of witnesses running alongside of us, sustaining us in the very difficult periods. We have also experienced in new ways the overwhelming love of God and the indescribable peace that passes understanding."

In October of 2006, Dante was hospitalized yet again. "My mother is on her way home to get some sleep. My Dad is at the hospital where his excruciating pain can be managed by the nurses," writes Andrea, one of Dante's daughters. Living 2,500 miles away in Vancouver, BC with her husband and children, Andrea could not be at her father's side. But she could send emails and in her less somber moments bring up the many memories she had of this man whom she so deeply loved. Michele, his other daughter, felt the same way. Both agree their dad played a big role, even in his sickness, in shaping their faith. "Over the last little while, I have talked to my dad lots about prayer," wrote Andrea. "The power of it. I have been most fortunate to have been able to talk to my parents, run things by them, listen to their years of wisdom, begin to ask the right questions; so they are walking alongside us as well."

In remarks made at her father's funeral, Andrea said both she and her sister were probably rebellious teens, and that they didn't like sharing their dad with so many others. But over time she began to realize two things: Dante loved God and people, but he also deeply loved his daughters. Among other things, she said he taught her the power of forgiveness when he, her father, sat her down in her early 20s (as he also did with Michele) and asked her to forgive him for the things he had done that had hurt her over the years. "He was my dad, but he was also my spiritual mentor," she said. "Having him as a dad meant God was an experience and not a teaching." The father she had often been frustrated with as a child, when he was just finding his way, "became a man and father whom I loved and respected very much."

Often the love they shared was unspoken and expressed through small gestures and nods. Andrea was Dante's "go-to" person when it came to electronics or things mechanical. They spent many hours together figuring out how to make things work. She had an innate ability with these gadgets that her dad sorely lacked. Especially important to Andrea was the great love Dante had for her four children: Alexandria, Jonah, Zakaria and Samuel. Dante was "over-the-top crazy" about all of his grandchildren and had greatly impacted their lives.

Michele fondly remembers the early years in New York City and recalls how very difficult the move to Grand Rapids was for the whole family. She says she especially connected with her father around music. She played the violin, piano and guitar and her father would sit with her for long periods of time, listening to her play, telling her stories about the jazz greats he had known, offering advice once in awhile. "I started playing music around age seven. I always wanted to impress him." A highlight was when she was able to teach him to play a little classical guitar.

Michele also recalls her dad as a man with an eye for gadgets—pens, tools, toy cars, electronic devices—and loved tinkering with them. More than anything, she remembers her father's smile and open arms, always for her, no matter what. "My dad always amazed me. He was so bright and gifted in so many areas and he didn't even recognize it. My dad knew more about everything than anyone I've known." Daily reminding her of her dad are the gestures and words of her young son, Tobin Dante. "His spirit carries on. He left a little bit of himself behind in my son."

Most important for Michele is the fact that her father, in his last five months of life, was able to spend time with her infant son, to be able to lavish love on him, hold him and play with him. Everyone who knew Dante well knew how much he cherished his family; he professed that wherever he went.

After leaving Madison Square Church in 1996, Dante maintained contact with many friends and watched with interest as the church continued to grow. When he got out of the hospital in October 2006, he made his last appearance there and spoke a few words. "I stand before you today by the sheer mercy and grace of God," he said. "As many of you know, I've been battling cancer for more than two years." The lively man from years before was a little stooped and pale, still himself and yet not necessarily the Dante that had grabbed hold and helped to make Madison Square what it still is today—one of the largest, multicultural congregations in the denomination. "A couple of weeks ago, things had progressed to the point that the doctor told my wife and me that I have about four-to-six weeks to live. But I have rallied this week to the point that I am able to stand here before you. I know that it is the fervent prayers of people that have brought me this far. And we thank you from the bottom of our hearts for your prayers. Don't stop!"

Being a pastor, especially the pastor of a diverse and changing congregation, is not easy, Dante often said. He had fought some battles there but had also experienced many joys and triumphs. He had preached about the God who lived in the very marrow of his bones. "Moving from the brink of death to standing here today has made it more real to me now than ever before that none of us knows when we will come face to face with death. But we do know that we will."

Dante was making his life and its current situation the subject of his talk. He dragged himself to the church in part to actually show people that death is real, its shadow looming always, and the key was how as a Christian to best handle it. "I know that when I do face the Lord, He will take me to be with Him because I have assurance of my salvation." He let that settle in, this reason why death for him was something he could handle. Then he asked, "Do you have assurance of your salvation? Are you sure where you are going when your life ends? Because when it's my time or when it's your time, God says, 'Ready or not, here I come.'"

In December 2006, Dante spoke about his state in a Christmas update. Using baseball images remembered from his youth as he watched his father playing baseball, he said, "Last year when they told me the cancer was gone, I felt like I had hit the seventh inning stretch, ready to go on with life. But now, it's the bottom of the ninth. There are two outs, but—but—the bases are loaded!" Aware that time was running out, he prayed that the pitcher pitched him a homerun ball that he could hit, driving in every player including himself to win the game.

46
TIME TO LEAVE

In February 2007 the family made the tough decision to put Dante into Hospice care. On March 2, he was sent to the Hospice inpatient facility because his pain was so out of control. An ambulance took him and Jackie there in a driving snowstorm. When he arrived, he was beat, but again he rallied and in a few short days became a favorite around the hospice facility. He soon knew all of the staff and they knew him. He told fellow patients stories, and once again began to think of writing about his own life.

Lying in bed or looking out the window, he thought back to the day he had the vision of the man rising in the middle of that Harlem street. He thought about how much he loved his mother and how abused she had been by her husband. But Dante also thought about the good things his dad did—like reading poetry on his own radio program, cooking a wonderful spaghetti sauce and polenta. Dante even typed up a bit of his story on his computer but got stuck when he wrote about his mother. He felt such pity for her having to do abortions to fund his father's schemes, which normally involved buying some bar or another. He didn't have the strength to write through that part for a while. All he could do was hurt for his mom. So he passed over it and recounted his time on the streets, ending everything with a detailed description of his conversion in jail.

Oddly, says Joel Huyser, Dante's life stopped and yet began there in that jail cell. The conversion was real and led him into another life altogether. Conversion meant for him a total and lasting turn around. "On one hand his story is one of triumph, but on the other hand there was tremendous cost to Dante for breaking the barriers he did and being the preacher that he was."

Once Dante started to feel better, he told his wife it was time to leave. This was a place for dying. "I have so much work to do. I need to get out so I can continue mentoring young pastors."

Dante walked out of the Hospice on a beautiful spring day, aware more than ever that he was coming closer to being with God. Life was sweet even when bitter. Back home, his moods shifted. He loved sitting in his room in the basement and playing records of some of the jazz musicians he had known: Miles Davis, Charlie Parker, Jimmy Heath, Thelonious Monk, Art Blakey, and Ismael Rivera. He had met them all, liked some and didn't like others. He spent time behind bars with a couple of them. He would let their music flow through him, taking him where it went, carrying him closer to Heaven.

Of all the things in his room, the most important was not his large collection of records and books. Rather, it was a large drawing of Jesus that he placed front and center on the wall so he could look at it often. "He wanted Jesus to be central in everything—even in his room," says Jackie. Over the years, he had spent many hours in that room: listening to jazz, salsa and Gospel music, preparing sermons, reflecting on what the Scriptures meant to his life, and spending much time in prayer and Bible study. "I love the Bible, man. It's all in there," he said, not long before he died. "Some passages I read again and again and get more out of it each time I read them."

Asked if he had any unfulfilled aspirations, he was quick to say that he did. "I'd like to start a multicultural church where people are able to see one another for who they are," he said. "I'd like to see blacks and whites and Hispanics and Asians together. Baby, that is what I'd like to see happen. It would be a church that teaches that God is integrated and not diffuse. Our God is the God of color and of change, and I like that."

Even as his health failed, he kept up an almost constant conversation with God. It was as if Jesus, the man/God in that picture, was at his side, a friend to whom he could speak about anything at any time. His relationship to God was more real to him than the cancer that kept showing up in different parts of his body and ultimately the doctors couldn't cure. From the time of his conversion, Dante had developed and nurtured an intimate, powerful prayer life. He was used to having familiar conversations with God. Even so, in times of intense suffering, it was difficult to pray. He then was comforted by knowing that others were praying for him, standing in the gap for him.

Death is a great destroyer, but it is not stronger than God. On his final visit to Madison Square Church, Dante wanted the people to know this in their hearts. He also wanted them to know why he was there. He was a witness to the stark reality that every life is fragile and in danger. He was there to tell of the glory of God, in hopes others would do the same. "Think about this: If you know a power and a truth that is so real, doesn't it, shouldn't it, burn within you to share this with others? This is what we call witnessing—sharing the Good News of salvation. This is also the command of Jesus: Go and tell."

Papa and Zakaria upper left, Jonah upper right,
Samuel middle left, Tobin lower left, Alexandria above.

47
"I WILL TRUST IN THE LORD UNTIL I DIE"

Dante's condition kept getting worse. It was very painful for his friends and family to watch his decline. "Just a brief update," Jackie wrote in an email in April 2007. "For the last day and a half, Dante has been totally unresponsive. And so we keep vigil at his bedside, thankful that we have been able to keep him at home with the help of many volunteers." Many times over the years, Dante had requested this. "I don't want to die in any type of institution. I want to die at home." His family, with the help of friends and the Lord, was able to honor his wish.

Rosie Hair, a social worker at a neighborhood community center in Grand Rapids, was one of those who visited Dante at home in his last days and with the assistance of others had prayed for him, often at length. Rosie and Dante had been friends and it was hard on her to see how this vital, passionate man had been ravaged and depleted by cancer. He had lost weight, the luster had gone out of his eyes, and bruises covered his body. By looking at him, she knew his fight was nearly over. Her heart hurt because she knew how much he loved life and there was so much ministry yet that Dante could have done.

Having spent many hours in conversation and prayer with him over the years, Rosie knew Dante's story and knew, as she watched him dying, that a powerful, spontaneous spirit would be removed from this world when he died. She especially knew how hard he had battled his own self-doubt that stemmed from his violent childhood. They had spoken often of bad spirits and of the demons that afflicted people, and of all the ones Dante had faced in order to be the minister he was.

Standing near his bed, she remembers being pleased, even in the midst of so much sadness, to know that on the journey over the last few years, Dante had been able to embrace and forgive himself, bringing on a new level of peace. "He could forgive others, but he had such a hard time forgiving himself." Rosie also thought of how Dante was like a diamond that, when viewed in the light, is a thing of beauty, purity and has many facets. With so many aspects to him, he could easily cross different cultures and barriers. Or in Dante's parlance: **"I can dance on many sets."**

Dante's living room was filled with family photos, Christian art and Bible quotes. Christian music played in the background. Years earlier he had said, "When I'm dying, I want to be surrounded with God's Word." A few close friends made quiet visits to the home. Mostly, his wife and daughters made the vigil, filled with sadness and great love for the husband/father/preacher who lay dying. Oddly, the room felt a little bit like Heaven even before Dante died. There was a gentle peace and softness in the air, a sense of completion and of new arrival soon to come.

Dante was quiet and unresponsive. But music and singing had been as much a part of him as words. Having been almost totally still for two days, Dante's lips began to move and his eyes opened as Jackie was quietly playing his signature chorus on the nearby piano. It was the song he had sung so many times and turned into one of the things that people knew him by: "I Will Trust in the Lord until I Die."

When she finished, Jackie rose from the piano, went over and cradled his head in her arms as his daughters held his hands. His lips stopped moving and his eyes closed as he took his last breath. He died about noon on April 13, 2007.

48
ALL FOR AN AMEN

Once the word spread quickly of his death, Jackie and her family were deluged with condolences. "He was a great visionary. He never drummed attention for himself or his needs," wrote a member of the community.

Bob Reed (d. 2010) and his family were working in Liberia as missionaries from Madison Square CRC when they learned that Dante had died. They praised how well he had handled the struggle with cancer and that his example served as a contrast to the way in which most people today face death—with denial. Dante did not like the cancer, wrote Reed, and even raged against it, but he "loved life, lived passionately. He fought with life and he fought with suffering and in doing so, he showed us a better way."

A former parishioner reflected on Dante's uniqueness. "If you were with Pastor Dante for even just three or four minutes, you didn't want it to end. His infectious laughter, his incredible personality and the great wisdom that rolled easily off his lips were inspirational. I wanted to hear everything he had to say. He was like E. F. Hutton. When he spoke, people listened."

In Dante's cancer journey, many of his medical professionals were drawn to his charismatic personality and the way he related to them. After his death, one of them reflected on Dante's life. "Dante was an icon. He was a gift to humanity."

Once Dante died, it was, as Rosie Hair predicted, as if a rambunctious spirit had departed his household and the world. He had been a walking storm and breath of sunshine for God, passionately bringing words to his thoughts, his beliefs and his love for the Lord. But then he was gone. A sad and empty silence filled the home. A man who exuded so much energy, laughter, power and influence was gone. Certainly, thought his family, Dante was in Heaven.

Years earlier he had told Jackie he pictured himself entering Heaven with great joy and crying out, "I want to see Jesus, for He's the one who died for me and set me free."

In a reflection on Dante, Jackie agreed that the departure of his spirit, which had been so large, left an empty, aching gap in their family. Yet, that same spirit, and this is what they would remember in the dark days ahead, "was irrepressible, and his ebullient, charismatic personality seemed too large to be contained in one body. It was too large to be confined to one culture, one New York City borough, one church, one denomination, one job or one profession."

In many ways, the image they like to keep in mind is of Dante exuberantly preaching. About 11 months before he died, he had the strength to preach his last sermon, delivered at Grace for the Nations Church. It was a sight to behold, say those who were there. Dante recounted his childhood, the problems he had faced, and especially his conversion. "How does a sinner talk to God?" he asked. Toward the end of his sermon, he summarized God's work in his life.

> "'If any man be in Christ, he is a new creature; old things are passed away; behold, all things are become new.' (2 Cor. 5:17, KJV) So my identity is no longer Spanish Danny; they call me Pastor Dante. I've got a new role model; he's no longer Sonny, but Jesus said, 'I'll be your role model.' I've got a new mind; I have the mind of Christ. Hallelujah! I've got a new heart. Hallelujah! I've got a new spirit. Hallelujah! I've got new freedom. Hallelujah!" (*The Testimony*)

He gave this sermon to a standing, whooping, arm-waving crowd. Listening to him preach, Pastor Tarence Lauchie', the church's pastor, referred to him as "an African warrior for God." Pastor Dante was a powerful man, with a powerful message. "Everywhere he stood became his pulpit, and every life he touched will never be the same."

Pastor Dante's funeral was held in that large undenominational church in Grand Rapids. People filled the pews. One of them was Rev. Phil Apol, then a Hospice Chaplain, and another of the ministers Dante had discipled. Apol still thinks often of all that Dante taught and meant to him. "Dante was a man and preacher who celebrated, with great and regular fanfare, the greatness and power of God. His ability and willingness to embrace and notice people, always by touching them, was unforgettable. Dante stood and walked with people, always available for prayer or visiting someone who was sick or in jail. He lived his life in the in-between places and often shed tears over things that were tragic and sad. But he repeatedly said, 'Phil, you gotta have fun doing ministry.' And he practiced what he preached. Humor was a tool he used, including in the pulpit. Laughter was part of his personality, and part of his theology."

On the evening of his funeral, there were those who believed that Dante had made progress to bring and sustain a truly multicultural church in Grand Rapids, especially in the CRC. He didn't take up the cause politically. He did it from the inside, from the ground on which he stood which was created and maintained by God. He sought and brought about change from the pulpit, not from a megaphone in the streets. His message was how he lived his life. Reconciliation was what this man who had overcome so much was all about: reconciliation between God and mankind first, then reconciliation between one another.

The people came to the memorial service to lift up the man and preacher who meant so much to them. In the end, Dante knew that multicultural ministry was hard and that true unity was a long way off. He knew that he worked the gate between the here and there. Everyone was in process and on a journey, guided by God, moving toward the final days when the Lord promised unification and glorification of all believers. Dante also knew one other crucial thing: The story is not over until God says it's over.

Dante's ministry had been for one thing and one thing only. Sure, there were lots of things to say and do. But it all came down to one thing. It was all that mattered. It was why he was put here, lifted from the gutter and then called by God to preach the Gospel. It was all for God, for His glory and a sign of gratitude for His providence and absolute sovereignty. It was for teaching people about Christ and His transforming, unifying love. From his childhood, Dante had to keep walking through flames, before and during his ministry, but he never stopped long enough to be consumed by the fire. In some ways, the fire helped to purify him. But in the end, Dante turned his back on the Inferno and kept moving forward, his eyes and heart on God. He rose above the pain and had many triumphs and joys.

The world, including the church, remained far too divided for this black Puerto Rican preacher man from New York City. Yet, he held on to his God-given joy. Ravaged by cancer and the pain it caused, he was able to muster a smile, a joke and even a few words of encouragement to friends and members of his family. He never stopped hoping or believing and kept telling anyone who would listen about the miracle that became his life. He knew he had come so far by grace alone, and his response could only be gratitude to God.

Ultimately, after all, it was All For an Amen!

Photo by Don Brooks Photography, used by permission

Andrea's family
Back row, l. to r. Alex, Jason, Andrea, Jonah
front row l. to r. Zakaria and Samuel

Michele and Tobin

Photo taken by Marie Clark Photography, used by permission

A WIFE'S REFLECTIONS: WINGS AND ROOTS

If someone had told me during my teenage and young adult years what God had in store for me, I would have been incredulous. How would it in any way be possible that I would marry a man named Dante Alighieri Venegas, with an alias of Spanish Danny? The turn my life would take and the journey that God would call me to were beyond anything I could have imagined. Such an unlikely story! But in retrospect, there is no doubt that God brought us together, bonded us together and blessed us together.

The Lord lifted Dante from the "guttermost" of life. Raised in anger and chaos, he endured emotional and physical abuse, rejection, and feeling abandoned when his mother was taken away. He experienced the horrors of heroin addiction, crime in the streets, homelessness and sleeping on roofs. He knew police brutality, injustice in the justice system and the threat of dehumanization in the prisons.

My life, in comparison, was calm and well ordered. I was brought up in a supportive, stable and family-oriented environment that emphasized education. It was a sheltered world, one in which our home, church, school and social lives revolved in Christian Reformed circles. My father was a Christian Reformed minister, which entailed moving when the Lord called him to five different churches. Although living in different towns in Iowa and Michigan, the social structure remained the same. My biggest challenges were the moves and a serious case of mumps at age 10 that left me hearing-impaired, greatly impacting my life.

Dante's Puerto Rican culture and my Dutch culture were worlds apart. Our personalities were also radically different. Dante was poetry; I was prose. He was jazz; I was classical. He was life-learned; I was book-learned. He was noisy;

I was quiet. He was charismatic; I was shy. He was ADHD; I was organized. But as we built our life together, we grew to accept and affirm each other's style. We both thrived in this cross-cultural environment.

Even so, we went through difficulties. When people saw us together, many assumed we would have problems because of our differing racial backgrounds; we did endure discrimination, which presented itself in many forms. However, our greatest difficulty came from the chasm between the subculture of the streets and my sheltered upbringing. At times, it was an agonizing process. But in working on our relationship, we focused on the God who had called us to this journey. A cardinal principle of our marriage was a Danteism: "We can agree to disagree on everything except the Word of God." Dante was an energizing force for me; I was a stabilizing force for him. He gave me wings and I gave him roots. Two opposites brought together and sent into ministry! Over the years, we often laughingly exclaimed, "Who could have imagined this scenario? God sure knows how to fix it, doesn't He?"

Our life together began in the boiling cauldron of multiculturalism in New York City. Our marriage grew there while Dante worked as a mental health counselor at Brookdale Hospital. We were blessed with two daughters, Andrea and Michele, both born in the Bronx. A bit later, we moved to Brooklyn, living near Brookdale. Their father was so fond and proud of them; they became his sidekicks. We spent a lot of family time together. Despite some difficulties, our lives were filled with much laughter, playfulness, adventure, music, wonderful relationships with many different types of people, church/school activities, and much love. Dante always had something going on!

Moving in 1978 to the small city of Grand Rapids, a quiet place with little connection between its various groups, was a very difficult transition for us. We found ourselves suddenly cut off from all things Puerto Rican: food, family, customs, and music, as well as New York City itself. For Dante it was such a seismic shift that his knees buckled, feeling as if he had moved to a foreign land. Finding a way of thinking and speaking so radically different from anything he had experienced called forth every ounce of inner strength to hold on to his calling. Both of us were so shaken that we nearly lost a grip on who we were. When his 40-hour, 9 to 5 workweek changed overnight to more than 40 hours plus weekends, our family was under great duress.

In 1978 there was no talk of culture shock, no cross-cultural training either for us or for Madison Square Church to help in the adjustment. Upon arrival, we found ourselves in the spotlight. Dante felt an unseen but powerful pressure to "succeed" and to conform to local mores. All of this put a tremendous strain on our marriage. But in God's amazing grace, He brought us through those first few very difficult years.

While being faithful to the call to help build God's church, Dante became a much-loved Pastor. He brought to the pulpit a contagious joy in the Lord and a new perspective: that of a slave set free. He knew what slavery to sin was about. Those cold, steel needles and mounds of white powder had enslaved him to a relentless master that was sucking the life force out of him. So when freed from that bondage, he surrendered to a new Master—Jesus Christ. "Dante, slave of Jesus" and "Dante, chief of sinners" were frequent self-descriptions. Often in reflecting on his life, with tears in his eyes and shaking his lowered head, he would say to me, with great angst in his voice, "I was soo, sooo lost! I was lost, lost, lost!!" From the pulpit he testified: "When a slave is set free from his bondage, do you think he just walks around slowly saying, 'Ho hum. Yes, this is nice?' NO!! He comes out walking and leaping and praising God!! The experience of freedom is overwhelming and he needs to respond. I've been called 'crazy' because of my exuberant worship style. If this is 'crazy', then I guess I am crazy. I'm crazy in love with Jesus!"

In journeying through life with Dante, I traveled with him in the streets, rehab centers, prisons, AIDS wards, hospitals, restaurants, many kinds of homes, in the multi-denominational and multicultural church scene. I was amazed at the scope of his ability to relate to all kinds of people and how he could so easily turn regular conversations into Gospel conversations. He frequently spoke of his special concern for "the addicted and afflicted, the non-descripts and the ne'er-do-wells. These are my people." And these were the people he spontaneously brought home for dinner or a time of respite. Since the Lord had lifted him from the gutter, he wanted others to know that in God alone there was hope.

Living at the cusp and clash of cultures challenged me to expand my horizons. I learned so much, just by being with Dante. Two truths, especially, came alive for me. First: The other person's perspective is just as valid for him or her as mine is for me. Second: Some of the most profound insights into life and the human condition come from those considered "the Least, the Last and the Lost."

I am grateful to God for calling me to be Dante's wife, his partner in life and ministry. It was a challenging, mind-opening world as I began seeing life through a multi-dimensional prism. For 40 years I witnessed up close the transformation of a new, unstable Christian into a man of strong principle, great spiritual depth, profound wisdom, and unshakeable faith; a man maturing from Spanish Danny to Pastor Dante.

Since his death, I've been asked, "What was it about Pastor Dante that made him special to so many?" That was also an important question for me. In the midst of my grief journey, a frightening moment arrived when I felt I was slowly losing my grip on feeling the essence of his personhood. Desperately wanting to capture that essence before it became only a memory, I began writing, and this document is what flowed from my pen. What the pen could not re-create were his supercharged energy and his repertoire of sound effects.

~

Dante

Dante Alighieri Venegas could turn any type of occasion into an event, just by showing up. Things changed when he entered the scene with a magnetism owning every room he was in. He was described in many ways: authentic, loving, forgiving, non-judgmental, passionate, creative, brilliant, impulsive, bold, fun-loving, a jokester, uproariously hilarious, radiated warmth, the real deal, transparent in the pulpit, willing to confront, streetwise while deeply spiritual, old-fashioned yet relevant, resolute in adversity, an indomitable spirit, an encourager, a bridge-builder, a poetical soul, a laughing warrior, a master communicator, a riveting preacher—impossible to categorize.

So what was it about this ebullient, charismatic Puerto Rican that endeared him to so many? Maybe it was his gregariousness; or his famous, loud, contagious laugh; or the twinkle in his eye and his welcoming smile; or his joyous exclamations over good food. Maybe it was his way of talking to people that made each one feel special. Maybe it was his comedic timing, along with facial and body expressions, reminding many of Bill Cosby. Maybe it was his vocal imitation of a bass player, saxophonist, trumpeter, a Thelonius Monk chord, an Ella Fitzgerald scat, an Ismael Rivera salsa tune—all while moving his hands and body to complete the imitation.

So what was it about this man? It could have been the comfort of his Pastoral heart in a moment of crisis; or the impassioned words of his beautiful and powerful prayers; or the great compassion flowing palpably from him in the hospitals, funeral homes, streets, prisons or any other painful, difficult life situations.

So what was it about this man? It could have been the way he bounded up the steps to take the pulpit while breaking exuberantly into a song; it could have been his sonorous voice, the lilt of his cadence, the hint of a stammer as his word production needed to catch up with his fast-moving mind; it could have been his soaring rhetoric as his whole body was pulled into action while making an impassioned point.

So what was it about this man? This could only be a man into whom God had deposited many gifts as well as a personality larger than life; a man whom God had rescued from the hands of the enemy and snatched from the fire. This was a man called by God and spared as he went through great tribulation before being brought out of the kingdom of darkness into God's marvelous light. This was a man whose track scars in his arms were redeemed by the nail scars in the hands of Jesus. This was a man who never took credit for anything but would, with great joy, give all the honor and glory to God alone for what He had done.

~

After his death, many have asked, "How was Pastor Dante able to overcome?" His firm assurance: "I know that I know that I know I'm saved." When he prayed in ignorance and desperation "To Whom It May Concern," out of all the gods he had sought deliverance from, the only one who answered was Jesus—the One who had fully paid for all of his sins with His precious blood and freed him from the tyranny of the devil.

He also had many strategies. But the most important were spiritual, especially Scripture memorization, prayer and praise. Learning "How do I deal with temptation?" and "What do I do when I sin?" were crucial elements. Did he struggle with sin and temptation? Yes, he did. He knew he was a sinner! And that he, like everyone else, could be tripped up by "the sin that so easily entangles us" (Heb. 12:1, NIV). For someone coming out of the depths of depravity and moving into an unfamiliar life style, learning **how** to live this life was of the utmost urgency.

Brutally honest with himself, he wanted God's Word to confront his sin. He could not afford layers of unconfessed sin and guilt to be built up. Genuine confession, repentance, and forgiveness—from God and toward others—took a central role in his Christian walk. He also dressed himself spiritually with the whole armor of God (Eph. 6). "God picked me up from the streets of New York City, dipped me in His cleansing blood and sent me out to the front lines," he explained. Fearless in sharing the Gospel, the word of his testimony rang with authenticity. God turned his street boldness into a holy boldness.

Crucial to Dante's testimony was his humble spirit: "Without God in my life I'm not worth two dead flies." His humble prayer: "Lord, keep your manservant hidden behind the shadow of the cross so You may be seen." His letter-closing phrase: "In His Grip." And in one of his many marked-up Bibles he highlighted

I Thess. 5:24 (NIV). "The one who calls you is faithful and **He** will do it." In the margin, he wrote "AMEN!"

As I reflect on our incredible journey, my mind returns to our meeting in early 1967. I was immediately struck by his warmth and engaging smile. Although neither of us was interested in the other, God worked behind the scenes for the next several months. Our first unofficial date was sitting by the Hudson River at 125th Street, discussing Scripture. The relationship grew very slowly, surprising us with a love that led to marriage. Through all our trials, our love deepened into an inseparable bond. A few weeks before his death, I received his last Valentine's Day card, summing up our love story: "My reason, my truth, my spirit, my love—Our God and you!"

The loss of Dante's presence has created a deep wound of grief for me, our children and our grandchildren. Wherever he went, he professed his love for his family. In God's mercy, He has gifted us, not only with our own memories, but also with testimonies from those whose lives Dante had touched. He made Christianity real and practical by teaching how to put theory into practice. His non-judgmental attitude helped set many free. And for many, far and wide, he remains a symbol of hope.

I still remember, with a sense of wonder, how people left the Memorial Service on the evening of April 20, 2007 lifted up on the wings of praise. The same spirit of praise that had characterized his Christian walk transformed the funeral into a celebration of the glorious overcoming victory available in Christ Jesus. Ringing in their ears were words from Dante's last sermon, summarizing God's work in his life and then giving his final challenge: "I just want you to get to know Jesus; that's all I want!" With the victorious strains of the *Hallelujah Chorus* filling the auditorium, there was no doubt that the glory of God had been manifested in the service. And all God's people had said "AMEN!"

The life of Dante Alighieri Venegas
—Rescued by God, Restored by God, Recycled by God—
Indeed had been
ALL GRACE, ALL TO THE GLORY OF GOD
And
ALL FOR AN AMEN!

Jackie Venegas

Vancouver, British Columbia

Dante's Sense of Style

Dante had his own sense of style and was a fastidious dresser, just as his father had been. Even as a kid, he always wanted to be "stylish." He was very particular about the quality of his ties; they had to have a certain feel so he could fold them correctly and make the right kind of knot. He knew what he liked but had a hard time coordinating things. So he requested, "Please don't ever let me go out looking like a clown." Or another favorite way: "Please don't let me go outta here lookin' like 'Whodunit.'" Over the years, he began to master the art of dressing. He would come to me, speaking with a questioning look that said, "How did I do?" When I gave him the thumbs up, he'd break into a long and hearty laugh, exclaiming, "You have taught me well!"

Sundays brought special challenges, as there was the pressure of time. Having difficulty pulling things together under pressure, he needed assistance from me. When I thought everything was finally together, I would sit down at the kitchen table to take a breather. He would hurry past me, ask for a last lookover and go to the car. "Well, I guess I can get myself ready now," I mused. Just as I would be ready to swing into action, he often came running back into the house, spinning through like a tornado, leaving papers and other things flying in his wake. Racing into the bathroom, he grabbed his cologne, put it in his hands and came racing back through the kitchen while slapping the cologne on his face and saying, "My public! My public!" As he jumped into his car, I collapsed into my chair: "Whew! I need a minute to get myself together here!"

Dante and the Roaches

Both Dante and I hated roaches. He feared them climbing up his legs, jumping onto his food, or crawling over him during the night. Even though the exterminator made his rounds regularly, they were never totally under control. If he saw even a baby roach, he went into action immediately, engaging in what he called "hand-to-hand" combat.

So it's not hard to imagine the scene when we entered our apartment in the Bronx after returning from Michigan following our wedding. We turned on the kitchen light and were greeted by at least 100 roaches scurrying over the floor and jumping off the walls. Dante screamed loudly and went running to the corner store to get some roach spray. The scene that followed would have been good for a movie. Our building was U-shaped; we were on the interior side, so our neighbors, a short way across from us, were able to see everything. They said it was quite a show.

Dante came running back in with the spray already flowing before reaching the kitchen. It wasn't too long before both of us had towels over our faces. The roaches stopped crawling and he heaved a sigh of relief. We ran to the window to put our heads outside for some fresh air. A bit later, we weren't even halfway turned around when he screamed again. The roaches were reviving from their stunned state and slowly beginning to crawl again. Some serious hand-to-hand combat ensued, accompanied by sound effects that added emphasis. He targeted one roach at a time, leaving it dying in a pool of spray. For me, this seemed to be taking too long while at the same time asphyxiating us.

In desperation, I began stomping on the roaches. He begged me, "Please stop! I can't stand hearing the crunch!" Since they seemed to congregate around the stove, we decided to look in and around it. When I opened the broiler, we discovered the previous renters had gifted us with a broiled hamburger that was still sitting in its own grease. Roaches jumped from everywhere, from every direction. This called forth a massive onslaught of roach spray with the administrator of the spray jumping so high and so fast to avoid coming into contact with them that one might have thought him to be a professional dancer. Finally, however, all roach movement stopped. The hand-to-hand combat warrior had prevailed. With screams and leaps, the roach killer had won the fight. But just to make sure, the next morning Dante quickly went out and purchased a roach bomb. He set it off in the apartment, necessitating our leaving for the day. Upon our return, not a roach was stirring.

Dante's Cross

Dante liked to challenge people with this optical illusion. "Do you think I can draw a three-dimensional cross with three unbroken lines?" When they didn't think it could be done, he would show them how.

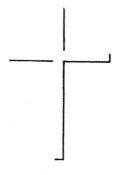

MORE DANTE

- ✟ **Timeline**   174
- ✟ **Writings**   176
- ✟ **Poetry**   185
- ✟ **Danteisms**   192

TIMELINE

1933 Born October 5 to Julio and Sara Venegas. Given the name Dante Alighieri Venegas. Born at home, 54 E. 115th St. in New York City's Spanish Harlem. Second of 3 children, first son.

1944 Family moved to the South Bronx.

1945 Hits the streets (12 y.o.). Smoking, drinking a little wine, hanging out, stealing—beginning the path toward drug addiction, crime and prison.

1949 Full-blown heroin addict (junkie). (16 y.o.)

1950 Drops out of Morris High School in the Bronx in his senior year. (17 y.o.).

1953 First arrest (19 y.o.). Arrested by FBI for altering a draft card. Sentenced to a year and a day; sent to the U.S. Public Health Service/Prison in Lexington, Kentucky.

1955 First arrest by NYC Police Department on May 4 for shoplifting. Convicted and sent to Raymond Street Jail in Brooklyn.

1957 Second arrest by the FBI. Arrested for stealing and forging checks. Served 3 years in Lewisburg Federal Penitentiary in Pennsylvania.

1953–1965 In addition to the above, over 18 arrests on small charges such as possession of narcotics, shoplifting, petit larceny. Did short amounts of time, such as 1 month, 3–6 months in various NYC penal institutions. Several cases dismissed.

1964 On May 2, arrested for an armed robbery he had **not** committed. Placed in Bronx County Jail. Conversion experience occurred on May 5. Faced 40 years. Case plea-bargained down to a year and a day. On July 30, transferred to Rikers Island. Acquired his GED.

1965 Released from Rikers Island in July.

1966 Signed himself in at the U.S. Public Health Service in Lexington, Kentucky for his last cure. Between 1953 and 1966 did 3 cures at Bernstein Institute in NYC, 3 cures in Lexington, KY, and a stint at Manhattan General Hospital. Also kicked cold turkey alone.

1966 After returning from Lexington, worked at a Post Office in Manhattan, then as a doorman for the 5th Ave. Lord and Taylor Dept. store.

1967 Hired by Addicts Rehabilitation Center (ARC).

1967 Met Jackie Mulder.

1969–1978 Mental health counselor at Brookdale Hospital Department of Psychiatry in Brooklyn.

1970 Married his wife Jackie.

1971 First daughter, Andrea, born.

1972 Second daughter, Michele, born.

1978 In September moved with his family to Grand Rapids, Michigan to enter the Pastorate at Madison Square Christian Reformed Church (MSCRC).

1981 Ordination service on October 18.

1978–1996 Co-Pastor at MSCRC.

1996–1999 Chaplain at Alternative Directions in Grand Rapids.

1999–2002 Pastor of City Hope Ministries in Grand Rapids.

2002–2007 Chaplain at Health Intervention Services in Grand Rapids.

2005 Diagnosed with Non-Hodgkins Lymphoma on January 13.

2007 Went to be with his Lord and Savior on April 13.

From **1953–1965,** Dante served time in 6 penal institutions. **Federal:** U.S. Public Health Service/Prison in Lexington, Kentucky; Lewisburg Federal Penitentiary in Pennsylvania. **NYC:** Raymond Street Jail (Brooklyn), Bronx County Jail, the Workhouse at Hart Island, and Rikers Island.

WRITINGS

Dante loved to write. He wrote to express himself, to entertain himself, and to examine his feelings. He wrote everywhere: at home, at school, in prison, on trains, on planes, in restaurants, in his study, and even in his hospital bed.

He always wanted to be ready when the muse spoke. He wrote on lined school paper, spiral notebooks, unlined paper, hardcover journals, small pocket notebooks, blank sections of newspapers, backs of used envelopes, restaurant paper napkins and placemats, and when it was available, good quality stationery.

His writing topics ranged from mundane, to humorous, to profound. He even wrote about his fascination with writing instruments.

My Fascination with Writing Instruments

There is something about writing instruments that fascinates me. Not just any writing instruments; rather, pens and pencils that have some unique quality about them. In some of these Quills of Quality, there may be one of several things that captures and transports me to the magical land of joy. For example, the weight or balance of any of these instruments; or the shape, the tip, the breadth of lines, the quill tip—gold, silver, copper, etc. Any one of these unique creations makes for immense fullness of joy and gratification for me.

There is also a combination of qualities that may contribute to the amount of fulfillment in my soul. Quite naturally, the basic function of the pen will automatically qualify it for entry into my world of dream fulfillment: the flow of ease in writing, the smoothness of the tip across a sheet of mute white paper, and the ease of switching from printing to cursive or cursive to printing. All of these are notable.

Writings from the Pivotal Point in Dante's Life

These were written before, during and after Dante's conversion experience on **May 5, 1964**. Three months of that time he was incarcerated in Bronx County Jail, then was transferred to Rikers Island to serve one year and a day. He had little knowledge of God or the Scriptures. His only source of information was a New Testament he found above the door of his prison cell that had been provided by the Gideons. There was no one teaching him on a daily basis. Years later he said, "The Lord was doing a crash course on me."

January 1, 1964

So I'm guilty of stealing from you? Yes, I stole from you.
But you know what? I'm guilty of stealing from myself.
Is that more important?

Ostracized am I? Haven't I already told you I've ostracized myself . . .
Five hundred x five hundred x for your five hundred pennies.

Care? Of course I care! But I care more for my reformation.
Then I won't be a financial threat to you anymore.

I'll be myself . . .
And wouldn't that be lovely.

May 9, 1964

I have debased the Ten Commandments, each one! I have defiled God's temple ten times ten thousand. I have committed every conceivable wrong towards morality and God. Am I not then a sinner? Yet I fear; even in my wrong I fear. God is Merciful. Yet I've abused His mercy and strewn about His grace. Am I not a Sinner?

Weak as man is, I have been the weakest. I pray for more strength! Tho' my outside world laugh, I —the inner not-self—suffer. Sinners have been forgiven, and I am a sinner. But a choice sinner, for I've committed all wrong and am a confused and repeated sinner. Am I to be forgiven?

May 12, 1964

A Soul runs rampant
Through the world of Illusion
And thereby misses the door of Life.

By Dante V. (God-inspired)

June 16, 1964

I'm well fortified here in my cubicle (cell). I have the Bible and the love of God. And each day that I step out, I feel to see if my Strength walks with me, for I have known weakness too many times.

And when I'm assured that He does walk with me, I walk on in faith.

Then I took more steps and went further from my cubicle, and again I looked around to see if my Strength walked with me. I was startled to find that in the confusion of the world and the newness of my Spiritual Birth realization, I could not sense Him.

Until I saw my Brother crying in his guilt and confusion. Then the Lord, my Strength, sent me to him. And we praised the Lord together.

June 25, 1964

Noise, Rioting, Drunkenness: the manifestations of the absence of Christ. And worth nothing. Yet too many men choose these evils to fill the void created by God's absence or negation.

To choose this course as a substitute is wrong. And a proven wrong; for man, being endowed with Christ-like qualities from birth, goes against his true desires by acts of whoremongering, drug addiction, alcoholism, idol worshipping. And always falls short of perfection and identification.

But man is never denied by God. Man has but to profess his desire to repent and purge his soul with Truth, and Christ offers man's prayers to the Father, and the Father in His graciousness saves man.

The Suffering Ceases.

June 27, 1964

If you do not like your life,
Do not seek to hide it in cards, games, or whoremongering.
Rather, be concerned for it, and cry for it—then pray.

June 28, 1964

Do you know who a drug addict is? He is "God's glory"—refused and confused by his ignorant negation of Christ Jesus. Martin Luther King Jr. is the opposite of a drug addict. The energy that Dr. King uses for the Civil Rights battle is the same energy and force that a drug addict uses to destroy himself, rather than build and glorify God. Take a drug addict, be kind and gracious to him, and show him his true worth. And you have a potential Martin Luther King. True man—God's glory.

June 28, 1964

I cannot share in your comfort and joy. For those things that you derive joy from are the very things I wish to escape from. Entertainment and joy such as yours will die and continue dying so long as it is from this world. I'm searching for life and I must practice and emulate the ways of life. Pardon me while I go to prayer.

June 28, 1964

Alcoholism—madness
Dope fiendage—madness
Whoremongering—madness
Card playing—folly
Gossiping—folly
Preoccupation with oneself—folly

June 30, 1964

If the Son therefore shall make you free, ye shall be free indeed.

John 8:36

It is getting very uncomfortable here in my imprisonment. Lately I've begun to think of my Freedom. After an incarceration of two months and ceaseless concern for the life of my soul and its deliverance, I've begun to think of something else—Freedom! Could this mean that my apprenticeship is over? That my limitations will soon be ended?

Perhaps this is it! After all, I was jailed suddenly and inexcusably under false accusations. Why shouldn't I be freed in the same manner?

June 29, 1964

The Indwelling Christ-like Spirit

Have you ever felt the power of the Holy Spirit? Do you know what it is like?

It is the unveiling of a new and better existence, after 20 years of an old and non-working hypothesis of life. A newness, a surge of Super Power. When I experienced it, it was so grand, so mighty, so all knowing and powerful, that I had to humble myself in prayer and ask for control and knowledge of the Titanic Force. I felt Super Holy, universal and above man's petty values. I was ready to heal the sick, to cast out leprosy. I felt like Jesus Christ.

I wouldn't speak for weeks. Conversations that were not directly concerned with Spirit were idle and useless, intrinsically un-edifying. I wanted to preach the Gospel to the whole world and I had never read one complete Book of the Scriptures. Yet I knew I could speak and tell of God's kingdom. I was and felt John the Baptist. I was the Holy Trinity yet I knew I was nothing. The Indwelling Spirit was the worker, and I only the vehicle for it - God's Temple. I first prayed that this feeling would not subside like so many other grand disillusions of mine. TOO TOO BEAUTIFUL!

I lost all personal values and gave of everything I possessed. I had no value for things of this world. I was so filled with the Holy Spirit, and it surged through me so strongly that the excess, the over-flow abundance of this feeling, manifested itself as love—pure love for all my unfortunate sinful, childlike brothers.

Once I thought the Holy Spirit was Joy and I wanted to experience it. But now I seem to be in almost constant mourning and everything unnecessary and cruel moves me next to tears. I have heard tell of people being baptized with fire. But I seem to have been baptized with Love, Concern and Truth.

All this happened and is past. Since then I've experienced many more things, and I am told by my Spiritual brothers that I will experience and witness more, for God has plans for my humble future. I pray for illumination thru Christ Jesus. Amen

July 6, 1964

There is another voice besides the obtrusive voice of guilt.
"Have you ever heard the voice of peace—Madman?"

July 19, 1964

Court Day
(Disappointed)

All the money on this earth could not have earned me a more beautiful lesson than the one I've learned in the past three months.

My mother is to be highly commended. The rest of my adored ones, the ones who held me in such high esteem and love, should "rot" in their hypocrisy! Strange how illusionary friends and families are. I would have given much for the love of my professed friends and loves. But now that I've seen their true worth in the darkness of my incarceration, I wouldn't give them much from my level, nor my mother's. Materialists all, strictly materialist and not deserving of anything spiritual.

The Reverend came to my rescue along with my mother. Two Christians. The word love should be relegated to spiritual people. They're the only ones who manifest true love. Because of these two persons' interest and love, I became aware of the dis-interest of all the rest. Thank God that in this world there are still people who do not profess love in words but reflect it in deed. God bless them, for theirs is truly the Kingdom of God.

Yes, in my darkness I became aware of a light, and the light mortified all evil and attracted Truth and Love.

July 19, 1964

The Truth

Forgive **you**? When you've accused falsely,
and never once admitted **your**
guilt . . . *Bodegero*?

Forgive **you**? When you arrest,
and turn me over to magistrates to
be persecuted . . . *Policia*?

Forgive **you**? When I'm slammed,
counted, and fed on **your** schedule . . . *Guardia*?

YES, I forgive, and thank **you**. This is my duty.
For you all have only done **your** duty.

My crime is not of the community
but rather one of Spiritual neglect
and my Punishment is my Salvation.

July 21, 1964

Hear that man singing.
He sings, he jokes and he spins many tales. He loves entertainment and he has many, and always, friends. Did you know that man is tortured by guilt and needs his noise because he doesn't know God?

See that man in silence.
He just left the man who's singing, and he don't want to hear no more! He knows there is a law he's missing, and the noise won't help him none.

Now watch that man who's praying.
I'll tell you what he does. He speaks to God and has no love for the world. He knows those other men, because he's been there too!

July 23, 1964

Prison Life

They offered us coffee kindly
    perhaps to pacify their guilt.
And I refused—I Don't Drink.

They spread joy in the Prison
    and gave out cigarettes.
Donated—Tax-free cigarettes.
    I Don't Smoke.

And they gave a movie, a comedy,
    perhaps to make us laugh.
But I wasn't happy.

Then when we laughed amongst ourselves,
    bothering no one . . .
They told us to be quiet!

July 1964

I stripped myself of Sin
Cast it upon the earth
Stepped on it
And brought my soul closer to God.

August 30, 1964

And when He (Jesus) passed on the Holy Ghost, He ascended into Heaven; for He had successfully fulfilled the Word of God. And He found himself in company with Abraham, Isaac and Jacob; also Saint Martin de Porres and many, many more men of God. And He tried to distinguish one from the next through association of color and race. But much as He tried and strained, He could not. They were all members of paradise, and equal rank was given to all.

For this was the eternal world of Spirit and Truth—Color was not known.

Sunday, Rikers Island

1965

After leaving Rikers Island in 1965, Dante visited his old church and was rejected. That sent him spiraling back into the darkness—the pit. His anguish is palpable here. He said of this year in his life: "No one was discipling me; no one told me how to walk in the Lord. That's my ministry—discipling men!"

During the days of my sin and seizure, I respected all spirituality. I even gave gifts to some gods who could deliver me from the snare I found myself pitted upon. I gave of the little I had in hopes someone, something would release me. I was hooked and escape seemed impossible; I looked to minor man and minor gods, and my woes bent me with weight.

Christ the Comforter, Jesus the Truth heard me, Bless His Holy name. Thank God for Jesus, who, full of mercy and understanding, heard me when my woes were about to tear me asunder. Jesus gave me life, He forgave my many sins. Bless Him.

Again I find myself slipping towards the pit. Death would be too soon; death may be too easy.

Lord, Lord, incline your ear to me. Lord, Lord, hear again my plight. I cannot defend myself against the enemy unless I fight with Your weapons. Guard me with Thy shield and buckler, Lord, lead me. I am blind and cannot see!

Send me light, Lord. Send me strength, Lord. Fight with me, Jesus! My enemies are looking to destroy; they're gaining ground, Lord. Come soon, oh God! Come now!

1965, A Lament

Oh God! Thou knowest my plight. Surely it is not new to You—You who have brought more tortured souls from their prison as You have already proved to me. Why then have You left me alone in the midst of deceit and debauchery, and even destruction? I babble words that reflect and beat me with their emptiness; cannot I contain myself in spiritual or holy silence? My pen is the only instrument silenced, and my lips pour out ugly words that are not accepted even in the pit of confusion. What is it, dear Father? Where must I begin? Restore my guide, dear Father. You who have the power and wisdom to stop worlds and begin universes; stop my babbling please, and begin my life.

June 5, 1980, Grand Rapids, Michigan

And who will believe my account? Witnesses?
Of course I have witnesses.

Ask the Devil who I was,
Then speak to momma, she'll tell too.
Ask my long-time friend from Harlem who has been a witness too.
And how about the untold friends who knew and loved me even
 when?

And then my Pastor, and now my wife
And the two little blessings who completed my life.
But who will believe it?—you ask again.
Then speak to the fruit—the born again.

As life progresses and we get older,
And man stubbornly clings to death . . .
I will raise up my eyes from whence cometh my help
And thank God for Life—The Breath!

Ask Jesus, the Holy Spirit, God—
    He is my only True witness.

Dante A. Venegas

POETRY

1954

This was written ten years before Jesus saved me.

>I heard my soul, and like a somnambulist
>I strode to pen and paper, and the paper spoke,
>   "Write!"
>Inhibitions must be torn down, respect must be
>   insulted,
>Shame trodden upon, if one is to be truly free.
>Then, yes then, enter humbly, to prostrate oneself
>   naked
>Before God. To receive, to be touched, blessed,
>   purged
>In that which is yours, and rise, to burst and
>   flow
>Like the pure, clear, cold virgin brook; eddying
>   forth,
>Forward to serve and sustain everything that
>   lives.
>Chanting as it moves on, murmuring across stones
>   and
>Slopes, refreshing, leasing, pushing, giving;
>And with a steady rhythmic pattern, chiming with
>   the World and all that nature ever gave. This is
>   purpose. This is freedom . . . this is God.

Written during the 'drug panic' of 1961; no drugs in the city, and I got a job in a vinyl factory in Carlstadt, New Jersey. It was physically demanding work.

1961

Ignorance of a Gift

"Look at my calluses," said the writer
    Whose fingers were a gift of God.
"And feel my muscles," he also cried,
    "And tell me if they're hard."

While the look upon his countenance
    Bore the look of a sentient saint,
The work he worked so hard at
    Was the lash for a gift grown faint.

1961

Softer, softer, Maestro, please.
    There's a dulcet note, shy and
So hard to find; but play, Maestro,
    Play, while my lyre and I struggle
To the accompaniment.

It almost sounds like love, Maestro—
    Eh? Love, did you say, Maestro, love?
Then play on. I should know the tune
    Quite well in spite of my limitations.

Love is a simple tune, a tepid melody
    Full of allegros and andantes
And sometimes long and abusive crescendos.
    Yes, I remember now . . . play on.
But wait, Maestro, the orchestra.
    Are we in key?

1964

Sara's Summa

Sara, who finds no task too big
   Nor any grace too small.
Sara, whose heart flings outward
   On the hinges of love.
Sara, whose Rock tolerance is
   The image and strength of woman.
Simple country Sara, whose sage
   Simplicity one must heed.
Sara, the worst Baker in the
   United States of America;
The worst shopper in the Discount
   Center of the world.
The most beautiful woman
   On the face of God's Earth.
                              Dante, her son

Dante's mother, Sara Hurtado Venegas

1964

I learned the mercy and grace of Christ
   To know and fear the law of God.
Then I trained in the law of God to
   Combat the world of sin.
Then I sent my soul-a-soldiering
   To bring Him back a medal.

       "There's Dante musing again.
          Let us invade his sacred ground;
       He will not insult us."

   (Commence the battle)

I drew my pen and slashed at paper,
   Desperately dipping from the well of saints.
I swiped error and salvaged truth,
   Then ducked the stones of man.

Armed with munitions of love and devotion,
   I wrote a poignant blow to the head of
My oppressors, and they stung me with
   Their guns of guilt.

I staggered to a pun, then a word,
   And when I thought all was lost,
The blessed arrows of angels sent them
   Running back to mortal man.

1964

   Once in a graveyard when I was
   A child, I heard a voice from below.
   "Coco, Coco," it pleaded, and I still
   Swear it came from below.
   Now as a man I no longer hear
   That distant voice from below.
   Instead, I hear the shrill whistle
   Of a bird upstairs, and I could
   Swear it's one I know.

1970

Brookdale Hospital
Department of Psychiatry

Black-bearded men toting degrees,
    Impulsively implementing theoretical
Values learned outside of inside—Lying!

Inside, black-people instinctively rejecting
    Outside values; indifferently fearful of
The unproven outcome of the income—Dying!

Staunch young strength! Repelling,
    Rebelling inside and outside;
Consuming; assuming leadership—Vying!

Young Jesus; absorbing "the thousand
    Natural shocks that flesh is heir to."
Knowing the pain, holding the balm—Crying!

1995

I wept in 1945 when President Roosevelt died.
I wept in 1963 when President Kennedy was shot.
I wept in 1968 when Martin Luther King Jr. was killed.
I do not weep for personalities, my friend.
I weep for the poor of the land
And for the splashing of blood
Of the heroes who dared to defend them.

November 14, 1992

Yesterday I died.
   Yesterday I died to all
The sermons I thought God
   Wanted me to preach to His people.

Yes, yesterday I died.
   I died to the need to please God,
Died to the need to please others—
   The more influential people in our church—
Died to the need to rescue others
   From their sin and guilt.

I died to the need to minister,
   To be seen, heard and accepted.
Yesterday I died—
   No, I was killed.

I was killed, and along with this killing
   I too killed.
I became a ghost, a killing ghost.
   A holy ghost that kills.

I am now a killer of pride,
   A killer of judgment,
A killer of self-deprecation,
   A killer of religiosity and
Sunday-go-to-meetin' clothes.

I kill my evil thoughts;
   I kill my evil and immoral actions;
I kill vengeance which is not mine.
   Yes, I am a killer!

Not only a killer, but also a ghost.
   I can feel but I cannot touch.
I can hear but I cannot speak.
   I can influence, I can reflect,
                           I can see.

Life

I think in Spanish
   And write in English.

I feel universal
   And act mundane.

I dream in vivid colors
   And see in black and white.

I hear in stereophonic
   And speak in monaural.

I learn incessantly
   And practice daily.

I live every day
   And die each year
      And die each year.

Death

Sometimes I feel,
Other times I merely reel.
Often I choose to see,
Yet at other times I just want to be.
Whether I feel, reel, see or be,
My yet one desire is to know
That I am always in Thee.
   Thank you, Lord.

Death is Dante's last poem, written in October 2006 in the Lacks Cancer Center.

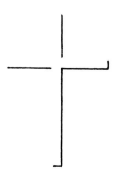

DANTEISMS

Dante was well known for his pithy statements—often humorous, but with an intellectual bent. Here are a few of them, both sacred and secular. Some are Dante originals, some are not, but he made them all his own.

~

Jesus, Jesus, Jesus.
Because His life is in my life, I have a life.
There is no life without Him living His life through my life.

~

I BELIEVE GOD.

~

Don't tell me what my God can't do!

~

God is God all by Himself!
He doesn't need you or me. He chooses to use us.

~

God said it, I believe it, end of story.

~

Without God in my life, I'm not worth 2 dead flies.

~

I want God's approval.
I don't care what anybody else thinks!
Period.

~

Learning that faith is based on the facts of God's Word
and not on feelings made all the difference for me.

~

I am governed by principles, not preference.

Don't unfix the fix that God fixed to fix you.

~

My God is able!

~

Secret sins: The truth will find you out.

~

This Book [the Bible] will keep you from sin . . .
OR . . .
sin will keep you from this Book.

~

It's not my job to convince people of their sin.
That is the Holy Spirit's job.
My job is to present the Gospel in love and leave the results to God.

~

I love God's laws and restrictions.
They provide the boundaries I need.

~

Being tempted is not the sin.
Yielding is the sin.

~

I was guilty of defiling this temple with opiates and "stupefications."

~

I don't believe in defending myself or making excuses.

~

Stand on the Word.
Stand means "don't move!"
Don't move off the Word.

~

Keep short accounts with God.

Pray with expectancy.
Be specific in prayer.

~

GOD IS FOR REAL!

~

Why do people hide their sins and confess their good deeds?
The Bible tells us to confess our sins and hide our good deeds.

~

Always leave room for a person to fail.

~

The only distinction with which I see people is:
Saved or Unsaved.

~

When I visit people in prison, I don't speak to them about the "what" and "why" of their crimes. I don't care about that. It makes no difference to me. The only thing I care about is the state of the person's soul. Prisoners are broken people, and they need hope just like everyone else. They don't need me to judge them and beat them up. They need to experience the mercy and grace that only God can give.

~

Just because you're *in* there (prison) doesn't mean you have to *be* there.

~

KEEP IT REAL!!

~

How far have you slidden in your hidden?
OR
Are you sliding in your hiding?

~

Flip the switch! (Change your negative thinking)

~

We become like those we spend most of our time with.
If 90% of our time is spent with non-believers,
our Christian life is seriously affected.

∼

What you preach in a very sound and practical doctrine,
I have experienced in a very powerful and experiential way.

∼

Develop an attitude of gratitude.
Even if you don't feel like it, begin praising God.
Praise is a spiritual weapon.

∼

Give thanks to God in all situations—even if it seems irrational.

∼

The Devil loves church. It's his favorite place to be.

∼

The Lord is my Shepherd; I shall not **W.A.N.T.**
Wander
Aimlessly
Near
Temptation

∼

Freedom or Free and Dumb?

∼

Don't get lost in the bayous of life.
Stay focused on your calling.

∼

Opportunity may knock once,
but temptation bangs on your front door forever.

∼

Death is the great leveler of mankind.
From birth, all humanity is on a conveyor belt,
Moving toward the inevitable end of each one's life.
At death, we all enter in through death's door,
The same way, on the same level.

~

In every volatile situation, death rears its ugly head for opportune finality.

~

I'm a Nobody,
not trying to be Somebody,
but willing to help Anybody
without losing sight of Everybody—
and always remaining me.

~

Father's Day: The Dad affects the whole family—
for good or bad, present or absent.

~

Would you like to be immortalized on celluloid?
(Have your picture taken).

~

"It's good to see you, Dante."
His reply: "It's good being seen."

~

"How are you doing, Dante?"
"Not bad for a black Puerto Rican from New York City
living in Grand Rapids, Michigan
and working for the Christian Reformed Church."

~

Always remember, the clown is often the loneliest person in the room.

~

If you snooze, you lose. You slow, you blow.

~

Give it to me straight! (Skip the details.)

~

You already have NO.
So go ahead and ask. You just might get YES.

~

My favorite sport? People-watching.

~

I can have fun all by myself!

~

In New York City you need a car that can hit and be hit.

~

Stay on the horse you rode in on.

~

Whose behavior can you change?
Only your own!

~

If you find a perfect church, please don't join it.
You'll mess it up.

~

He's been wrong so long that he thinks he's right.

~

I dislike those guys
who criticize
and minimize
the acts and deeds of other guys.

~

I get paid to talk.

~

I don't have a good memory; I have a trained memory.

~

I don't fit anywhere, but I can fit in everywhere.

~

I'm a Nuyorican.

~

Listen to this!

~

God's people are not to be
Bored or boring.
They are to go out boldly.

~

From needles to needless,
From pain to pleasure,
From bondage to birthday,
From the cross to Christ,
From slavery to salvation and freedom clothes.
Therefore, put off the old man with its lust and put on Christ.
Free at last. Thank God Almighty, I'm free at last!

~

Yes, I'm high! High on the Blessings
and wisdom of the Almighty.
And my Euphoria is not the nod,
But the Light of God's love!

~

To God alone be the glory for the things He has done.

~

Do not let any unwholesome talk come out of your mouths, but only what is helpful for building others up according to their needs, that it may benefit those who listen. *(Eph. 4:29)*

(Dante's message on the home answering machine)

May the words of my mouth and the meditation of my heart be acceptable in Thy sight, oh Lord, my Rock and my Redeemer. Keep your manservant hidden behind the shadow of the cross so You may be seen.

(Dante's prayer before preaching)

Now unto him that is able to keep you from falling, and to present you faultless before the presence of his glory with exceeding joy, to the only wise God our Savior, be glory and majesty, dominion and power, both now and forever more. Amen. *(Jude 24–25)*

(Dante's favorite benediction)

~

Remember that you were slaves in Egypt. *(Deut. 24:22)*
(My Egypt was The Bronx, Brooklyn, Manhattan)

Thank you, Lord, for deliverance from over twenty years of needles bondage to opiates, stupefications, and stimulants!

May I *never forget* the power of *your resurrection in my life* and the freedom you have given to me through the Cross of Calvary.

I'm yours, Lord—Bless Your Holy Name!

(Dante's last testimony, 2007,
written on the back of an envelope)

ACKNOWLEDGMENTS

Chris Meehan

This book on the life and ministry of Rev. Dante A. Venegas came, in many ways, from Dante himself before he passed away. He told me he had always wanted to write his story but was never able to complete it.

I wish to thank James Haveman for connecting me with Dante. He helped in many other ways, supporting me through this four-year process. He is the one who got the book off the ground.

Thanks to Jackie Venegas, Dante's wife, without whose recollections, memorabilia, and many hours of fact checking, proofreading and editing, this book could not have been written.

Thanks to Dante's daughters, Andrea and Michele, for their help by sharing their recollections of their father and his influence on their lives.

Thanks to Rev. David Beelen, pastor of Madison Square Church in Grand Rapids, Michigan for describing his co-pastorship and relationship with Dante. He also made available records from Church Council meetings, which proved invaluable in writing the book.

Thanks to Rev. David Sieplinga, pastor of Bethany Church in Muskegon, Michigan for sharing with me his crucial role in helping Dante enter the ordained ministry.

Thanks to Dick Harms, the archivist at Calvin College in Grand Rapids, Michigan for making available all of the documentation that the archives had on Dante.

Thanks to Andy Angelo, news editor of *The Grand Rapids Press*, who helped to edit and asked many important questions about this book. His support was invaluable.

Most of all, I wish to thank Dante himself for sharing his story with me and providing me with a partial autobiography he had written, recounting his early days. He also needs to be given credit for the title of this book, *All for an Amen*, because that was his idea.

For this project, I read as background several books and articles about life in Harlem and drug addiction in New York City during the time Dante lived there. I want to thank those authors as well as the many people—too numerous to name—who shared their recollections of Dante in interviews with me. Articles from *The Grand Rapids Press*, where I once worked, and from *The Banner,* the official magazine of the Christian Reformed Church, were also very helpful. Other valuable sources came from Dante himself: his journals, Bibles, writings, poetry, letters, sermon notes/tapes, and the CD of *The Testimony.*

The Venegas Family

The Venegas Family expresses our profound gratitude to all those who have contributed in any way to the publishing of this biography on our beloved husband, father and grandfather.

We especially want to thank Chris Meehan for taking on this project in unusual circumstances, with very little time left in Dante's life. We are thrilled that you were able to meet with him a couple of times. Although Dante was very ill, you were still able to get a sense of his story and of the person he became through God's grace and transforming power. We thank you for the dedication with which you have embraced this endeavor and honor you for fulfilling your promise to Dante that you would make sure this book was published. You have served him and us very well.

We wish to thank Shirley Neitzel for the many hours she dedicated to helping format this book. Shirley is a children's author. We so appreciate your willingness to help and to share your expertise with us.

We wish to thank Dan and Barb Malda for their help in inserting the photographs, designing the cover and preparing the book for printing. We are blessed by your excitement for the project and for your contribution to it.

We wish to thank Grace for the Nations Church for taping and transcribing *The Testimony*, Dante's last sermon. It has been an invaluable resource for this project.

As Dante's family, we lovingly thank Dante himself for the rolling commentary on the vast dimensions and aspects of his life, his wise insights into life in general and the deep spiritual wisdom that he provided over the years. Those experiences shaped us, and the memories live on.

Most of all, we thank God for His role in our lives together. We are blessed to have had the opportunity to witness first-hand how God works in powerful ways in the lives of people. And we join in on one of Dante's favorite exclamations. "To God alone be the glory for the things He has done."

Puerto Rico

Chris Meehan worked for nearly 40 years as a newspaper reporter, much of the time covering religion. After retiring from the news business in 2007, he became the news and media manager for the Christian Reformed Church in North America. He has written several books, including five mystery novels, histories of churches or church ministries, and a biography of John Calvin entitled *Pursued by God*. He lives in Grand Rapids, MI, is married and has four grown children.

Jackie Venegas is co-author of this book. She worked in the field of education in Chicago, New York City and Grand Rapids, MI. Jackie is the widow of Rev. Dante A. Venegas and worked tirelessly with him in various ministries throughout their 37 years of marriage. They have two daughters and five grandchildren.